Marketing
for
Mortage
Brokers

Marketing
for
Mortage
Brokers

A "How-To" on Trackable Direct
Response Marketing Systems

Scott Tucker

Published by Advantage, Charleston, South Carolina.
Member of Advantage Media Group.

ADVANTAGE is a registered trademark and the Advantage colophon is a trademark of Advantage Media Group, Inc.

Printed in the United States of America.

ISBN: 978-1-59932-096-0
LCCN: 2008943069

Most Advantage Media Group titles are available at special quantity discounts for bulk purchases for sales promotions, premiums, fundraising, and educational use. Special versions or book excerpts can also be created to fit specific needs.

For more information, please write: Special Markets, Advantage Media Group, P.O. Box 272, Charleston, SC 29402 or call 1.866.775.1696.

Visit us online at **advantagefamily**.com

Table of Contents

Introduction

What gets me most excited in life are all the opportunities that present themselves in our country to make money through entrepreneurship. I see no reason to live in America just to be the janitor at Wal-Mart. I think that's far beneath what anyone is capable of. Just about anybody in America can own their own business, they can make their own fortune, and they can come from nothing to create something for themselves. Education and economic background simply don't matter.

What does matter is what you do with the rest of your life. Your past and your present have nothing to do with your future unless you decide that they should. If you limit yourself by what your past or your present is, you're really doing yourself a disservice. What excites me most each day is getting that much further towards where I want to be as a person and in business.

In 1998 I got involved in the mortgage brokerage business in Chicago, working for a friend. We had a falling out at the end of 2001, and he threw me out on my rear, even though I had done very well for him. My first full year in business with him, as his loan officer, I was able to make $100,000, which was fairly unusual. I was only getting a 25% split with him, so, in 1999, I had actually generated over $400,000.00 in fees and kept $100,000.00 of that for myself; the rest went back to his company. In 2001, the year he let me go, I made $152,000.00 personally and had generated over $600,000.00 in fees for his brokerage.

That January I started studying direct response marketing, and researching all the old masters: Claude Hopkins' *Scientific Advertising,*

The Gary Halbert Letter, and I read a lot of Dan Kennedy's stuff. I bought courses and studied twenty-four/seven, including weekends. So for January, February and March I lived off of savings. Then I went out and got $100,000.00 of available credit, just in case, still with about $20,000 in savings. The first week of April 2002, I mailed out a five-thousand-piece mailing; it cost me $5,000.00, all in the hopes that the phone would ring.

Well, it did—in fact it rang like crazy for about a month. The phone calls just kept coming and coming. I had to work seven days a week, twelve hours a day, from Monday through Friday. On Saturday, I'd scale it back to about eight hours, and on Sunday, about four hours. That first $5,000 mailing brought back $75,000.00 in fees in the first 60 days, just because it took 60 days to close all the loans.

I was charged my borrowers top dollar, just like I had always done. I charged the legal maximum fee in Illinois, which is 5 points, and I got it. From there, I was off to the races. I was getting a 100% split at this point from a net branch company, so I paid them $500 per file, and got to keep the rest of the money. So, say, on a $12,000.00 fee, like the first fee that I had on my own, I'd pay $500 and get the other $11,500.00 for myself.

So out of that first $75,000.00 that I got back from that $5,000 mailing, which I had put on a Discover card to get started, I was able to pay-off that Discover card, and order another $5,000 mailing.

In the 10 years that I've been in the business, I've acquired a deep understanding of direct response marketing and all its uses. Whether it's through direct mailings, freestanding inserts, display ads, or the proper use of websites, nothing has taught me more than just doing it and learning what works and what doesn't. For example, most people think that websites will bring them all kinds of borrowers. That's really not true. Websites are great for taking people from offline to online, where you have unlimited space. But to get them online, you still need something like a direct response mail piece or a freestanding insert, or a display ad, maybe even a door hanger.

The educational materials I provide, outside of this book, are bundled into my mortgage marketing, coaching, and consulting membership program. You can find out more about that at www.MortgageMarketingGenius.com.

How It Works for Borrowers

The secret of my marketing system's astronomical success rate is this: the marketing I've created doesn't have to do with the product or service. It has to do with the homeowner.

When your average potential borrowers, let's call them Marge and Homer, read your mail piece—be it a freestanding insert, or a display ad in a niche publication, what have you—they don't feel that we're talking to them about mortgages. They feel we are talking to them about their problems, their agitations, and their emotions; and then we present them with a solution, the solution being ourselves, not a "mortgage refinance."

This ends up creating a sense of excitement from borrowers because they're happy to get rid of their past problems, but are also looking forward to the additional tax benefits we set up for them, and a credit repair sort of thing. They forget all about rates and fees; and in most cases, they don't even ask. Brokers and loan officers who use my marketing system, who are members of my program, find that 90% of the time, people never ask about rates, and 95% of the time they never ask about fees.

However, if they do ask, the answers are simple, because you've already gone through the list of problems, and not only solved them, but also added benefits. It's important to remember that the marketing never presented this as a mortgage refinance offer, so you usually never even have the rate and fee discussion. But if borrowers ask, "Well, what's the interest rate?" because that's the question they think they're supposed to ask—that's what *USA Today* and Ditech and all of them talk about—all you have to say is, "Well, the interest rate is only 8.5% and that's 100% tax deductible interest, which is what you really want, isn't it?" And, of course, it is.

If they ask, "What's the fee?'" you say, "The fee is only five (or 7.99 in un-capped states) points." And if they ask, "What does that come to in dollars?" you can tell them that, for instance, "on your $100,000 loan, it's only $5,000." They usually have no problem with that either—which may sound strange, but it works, because the benefits, as we've already presented them, outweigh any fee. There are also going to be instances of tax deductions of the points charged, which I would ask you to consult your CPA about.

How It Works for Brokers

My approach is to provide you with a marketing system that plugs into your business and operates on autopilot. I'll also educate you on the way you should present yourself to the marketplace so that you are congruent with the marketing that is provided. You should no longer think of yourself as a "mortgage guy" or gal who talks in terms of rates and fees; Your borrowers will not be concerned about rate and fee, so long as you can make your borrowers feel that their problems are being solved, their fears and anxieties relieved, and that they are actually excited about the outcomes that you are about to create for them. By talking about their problems and their emotions and so on, not only can you provide them with a solution, you then present them with benefits above and beyond what they had asked for in the first place.

When you talk to people about their problems and present yourself as the expert, you will get people to call you. And because you haven't had the "mortgage" conversation in the marketing piece, you will get people calling you that have applied nowhere else for a mortgage, or they've applied somewhere else with somebody who didn't have the sort of agility that a local broker would have. Or, they called Ditech and were turned down because they didn't fit within the box that the telemarketer wanted to put them in.

By creating marketing for mortgage brokers, I have freed up the time of my members who use the system. Members then have the mental energy, time, and focus to keep their attention on their borrowers, instead of having to learn about emotional direct response marketing themselves. They don't have to think about what list to use, or if it works, what selects to use to pull counts of the list, what list broker to use, what mail piece to mail, how to create a mail piece, how to create the envelope, or how to manage the logistics. All they have to do is use my system, in a plug-and-play manner. They just plug in their information and an entire mail campaign, or website, or freestanding insert is created for them. The display ad is already at the ready, and in template format. Of course, all my marketing pieces are copyright protected with the Library of Congress, so they do need a marketing license to use them, but that's included with my system.

In the Footsteps of Giants

Nearly 100 years ago, before Andrew Carnegie died, he commissioned a young man named Napoleon Hill to go on a 20-year journey to research the traits that all successful men had in common. His task was to put all those traits into book form, so that a young man or woman from a poor family could read the book and follow the plan that had been laid out by people like Henry Ford, Charles Schwab, and Carnegie himself. With Carnegie's introduction and calling card, Napoleon Hill was able to interview the most successful men of the time. That book, which Hill wrote without any financial compensation other than the rights, became *Think and Grow Rich*, which is referred to by more self-made American millionaires than any other as the book that changed their lives.

One of the strongest ideas within this book is the mastermind principle. This is the idea that you should have an association of people with like goals and like minds that help each other through the challenges of business, because everyone has blind spots and everyone has strengths. With a group of, say, ten people all of who have similar goals, you can all work on each other's businesses; or perhaps you all work on the same business together. That is the way to success, and in fact, I don't see how you can succeed without it.

The Tucker Mortgage Marketing System® provides you with that mastermind network. You can learn more about the Tucker Mortgage Marketing System® at **www.MortgageMarketingGenius.com**.

With my automated mortgage marketing systems that I plug these members into, I'm able to reduce their working hours, so that the average member in my program is only working 25 hours a week. That easily translates to about 5 or more transactions a month, at an average of 5 points apiece on each deal. Making that kind of money, while only working about 25 hours a week, and with all the grunt work automated, my members are very, very happy. They're able to spend time with their children, or their wives or husbands, whatever the case may be. *I'm* the one spending the time doing research for them, writing new marketing pieces for them, tweaking my system specifically for each member's area as needed; *I'm* the "marketing brain" so that my members don't have to worry about what's new in the industry, what's just happened that will change thing in months to come, or what marketing is working now to get you deals that pay big, fat commissions.

The purpose of this book is to get you thinking about the business that you're *really* in, which is the *marketing* business.

My Tucker Mortgage Marketing System® presents you to homeowners not as a "mortgage guy," but as the solution to all their problems.

Summary:

- All of your challenges in the mortgage business can be solved with proper mortgage marketing.

- It's possible to send out a $5,000 mailing, and make-back $75,000.00, in just 60 days.

- You need to know your state's fee cap. Many think they're in a 5-point capped state, when they're not; they could be charging 7.99 points, if they had the right marketing to smooth the sales process.

- You can get a 100%-split as a loan officer, if you know how to work a good net branch deal with a mortgage banker.

- Stop selling mortgages. Start selling benefits.

- You can automate your marketing and your inbound lead-taking process. Work less and make more.

- You can learn a lot from people outside the mortgage business. More than you can from those inside the mortgage business.

- You're in the marketing business, not the mortgage business.

Making it.

PROFILE: SCOTT TUCKER

BY SUSAN BOVE'

Still making a meager income after five years of service in the Navy, and after college, Scott Tucker moved from Michigan to Chicago, and invented his own path to success!

Growing up in DeWitt, Michigan, Scott Tucker's childhood "was pretty average." He was a mediocre student, who barely ever studied, and often didn't do his homework! "I spent my time playing hockey, lifting weights, and cracking jokes. I only did what I had to do to stay on the hockey team, and to graduate," Scott says.

They always told him that if he wanted to make something of himself, he had to go to college.

"What a bunch of crap!" Scott Tucker now says. "But I wish I'd known then, just how clueless, and full of it, all those school counselors were!"

As his high school years drew to a close, Tucker began to realize that college was not an immediate possibility for him anyhow.

"My family didn't have any money." And he'd goofed-off all through middle and high school. A class clown, high school hockey player, and weight lifter.

Examining his options, he decided to join the Navy. "Not really for the GI Bill,

just because I was sick and tired of classrooms! I just wanted to go *do* something! Not talk about more silly theories! I've always been an *action* guy," he says.

"I've always had a terrible case of 'attention deficit disorder.' I remember after second grade, I got bored and they could never get me to do my homework." Tucker says, "I think they thought there was something wrong with me! Maybe they were right!" he says.

Tucker thought the Navy's cryptology program (code-making and code-breaking) would give him a chance at a career in the FBI or CIA, after what he then thought would be a 20-year career in the Navy.

Because he didn't take the right classes, and get good grades in high school, Scott had to join the military as an enlistee, rather than as an officer candidate.

"That really didn't bother me, because I come from a blue-collar family anyhow. My grandpa was a truck-driver, dad's a handyman, and mom's a nurse. I didn't mind getting my hands dirty," he says.

Scott shocked half his teachers, and proved the other half right, when he scored so high on the Navy's recruiting test, that the recruiter showed up at the high school begging *him* to sign-up for the Navy's top secret nuclear power program.

"They really filled their britches the day those test results came in!" Tucker says. "But I wasn't surprised that I'd done so well...even though I had *never* done well on the *school's* 'standardized tests!"

"The military's test was about common

sense stuff. Not pointy-headed algebra kinda things!" he says.

"The recruiter, and his Chief, all of them kept after me until the day I left for boot camp...to go into the 'nuke' program, instead of cryptology! Because, that way, the recruiters would get double points!" Scott says.

"The cryptology program is one of two top programs the Navy has. It's that and the nuke thing. And they have just as hard a time filling spots in cryptology as they do with the nuke program, but the point system for the recruiters is all out of whack," says Tucker.

Tucker proved to be a model Sailor, and was selected for his command's Junior Sailor of the Year award out of about 800

continued on page 69

> *Anyone can get the kind of success that I now have!" says Scott, standing in the kitchen of his new custom home, "All it takes is a knowledge of emotional direct-response marketing!*

other Sailors.

He was also heavily decorated during his service, recognized by Rear Admiral Fallon, by his Captains, and others. Today, a "shadowbox" full of medals, ribbons, chevrons, and such hangs on the wall above his desk in his Roscoe Village neighborhood office.

Next to his medals, are his dad's, and his grandpa's. "Dad did a tour in Vietnam in '69 with the 4th Marine Division as a Navy Corpsman."

"Grandpa was a B-24 Liberator tail-gunner with the 8th Air Force in the Army Air Corps."

"Grandpa did the raids of the Nazi's Romanian oil fields, and wasn't supposed to make it through all his missions. I think it was about a third of the B-24 crews that lived through all their missions, and got to come home."

"Dad did his year in Vietnam, with infantry Marines. Helicopters he flew in crashed 2 different times during that year! Must have made it hard to keep getting back inside those things!" Tucker says.

"And, he hurt his back during that tour, trying to carry some 250-pound Marine on a stretcher. His back's still messed up today." Tucker says.

As for Scott, in the spring of 1996, just three months before Tucker's own Navy contract was up, he was told that he'd been selected to serve at the White House.

He had been planning to get out, to move back to Michigan, and finish up the college degree he had started working on during his time in the Navy.

Scott was on board the aircraft carrier, USS Theodore Roosevelt (CVN 71), in Norfolk, Virginia then. "I went in that morning, while we were in port, and my division officer had gotten a message that I was to report *the very next day* for White House interviews!" Tucker says.

"Everyone in my division was real happy for me. My Chief said he wished to

hell he'd gotten that chance! But I wasn't real sure how to feel...or what to think about all that," Scott says.

"Reason being, is I'd been planning for about 12 months to get out. And besides, it was March '96 when they told me. Bob Dole was losing the election, and I couldn't stand Clinton. And I sure as hell didn't want to work for him and Gore!" Tucker says.

"My chief just about hit the overhead when I told him I was gonna get out! He was really p.o.'d! I had this chance to spend the rest of my career at The White House, and was giving it up! No more transfers once you're there! No more 6-month cruises, and no more 20-hour days! After just 5 years I had this chance, when my chief was 13 years-in, and they'd *never* asked *him*!" Scott says.

"The White House gig wasn't optional if I re-up'd. That's the *only* place I'd be allowed to transfer to after the ship. They had put me on 'White House hold' with my 'detailer.' That's the guy who makes transfer assignments," Scott says.

"That meant that I couldn't transfer to Key West or whatever, after the ship, because the White House had me on hold with them." Tucker says.

"So I got out!" he says. Upon his honorable discharge in June of 1996, having served five years, Scott quickly learned that there were no openings for

"code breakers" in the civilian world. "It's kinda like being a sniper! Not much work on the outside for that!" he says.

Very little he had learned in the Navy actually applied to the real world. To support himself, he took the only job he could get hired for. He became a $7 an hour security guard at an auto plant in Michigan, where he'd grown up. "Man was that depressing! That was a real hard time for me," Scott says.

Miserable with life, Scott enrolled full-time in college, while still working full-time to support himself.

"I chose to finish my degree in business administration, because that's what I'd always been interested in." says Scott.

Once he had finished college though, Scott figured-out that his time in school would have been better spent working instead.

"If the theories my business professors

> **I am living the lifestyle I have always dreamt about. Once I figured out how to make my marketing work, the rest was easy!" says Scott, in his rooftop hot tub.**

taught *actually worked* when it came to making big money, they would have conquered the business world *themselves!* Not preaching to other people how to do it!" Scott says.

Then Scott got a job as a mortgage loan officer. But he still was *not* making the kind of big money that he really wanted, and felt trapped in his commission-only job, without full personal control of what he calls "lead

continued on page 70

MARKETING FOR MORTGAGE BROKERS

"I didn't know where next month's mortgage payment was gonna come from!" he says.

It was then that Scott cracked the code on mortgage marketing. While in his first month of going it alone, and working as a loan officer for a new company who refused to do *any* marketing for him, he was getting more leads in than he could handle.

"When I got canned from that other broker, I rolled up my sleeves and spent morning, noon, and night studying every single thing there was to learn about marketing! I bought every book, every tape set, you name it! I listened to, and read everything there was! I read stuff on marketing that had been written in the early 1900's! You name it!" he says.

"Now, I'd venture to say, there isn't any other mortgage broker in the country that has as deep a knowledge of marketing, and how to bring in a flood of leads as I do!" Scott says.

flow."

"Then, to add insult to injury, with *zero* notice, and exactly one week before Christmas, I was fired from my job!" he says.

"Sheesh! I was the highest-producing loan officer they had! Doing two-thirds of gross income for the entire company! It's just that I wouldn't put up with any abuse from my broker! I've never been good at

backing down from anyone's b.s.!" Tucker says.

"Even with so-so leads, and no control over how many, or what quality I'd get, I was closing everyone at the maximum fees allowed by law. And the borrowers all loved me." Tucker says.

After his sudden firing, and at age 28, Scott was unemployed and completely broke. With his back against the wall, and facing foreclosure on his home, Scott was forced to figure out how to make marketing work in the mortgage business.

What Scott had developed was several systems that employ what he calls "emotional direct-response marketing." These are what he credits for keeping leads flowing into his business morning, noon, and night. "Without me being on call like some idiot 'Realtor!'" he says.

"Back then I was forced to find a way to market myself that would bring in big wads of cash *'yesterday'!* Little did I know, I would have more work than I could handle!" he says.

"Now I never work more than 40 hours a week! My marketing systems allow me to work smarter, not harder!" Tucker says.

> ❝ *Now I never work more than 40 hours a week! My marketing systems allow me to work smarter, not harder!* ❞

Scott Tucker is available, on a limited basis, for consulting work with a select clientele of business owners, in several different fields. For more information, fax his office at (773) 327-2842.

Chapter One
The Mortgage Industry Today

As I'm writing this book, it's fall 2008, and the current state of the mortgage industry is one of worry, doubt, and frustration. A lot of folks in the business are questioning if the business will ever come back, or how to make money in the current market. As Napoleon Hill said, "In the ashes of every defeat lie the seeds of equal or greater opportunity." And so every mortgage market change, downturn, fluctuation, or what have you, creates new, and oftentimes better, opportunities for the mortgage broker and/or loan officer.

Some current opportunities that exist in the marketplace are reverse mortgages. Because of demographic changes and so on, "baby boomers" are becoming eligible for reverse mortgages, as the borrowers only have to be 62 years of age or older. Since the borrowers can be helped by a reverse mortgage, even when *already* at 85 LTV on their "forward" mortgages, reverse mortgages present us with a huge opportunity. Members of my program have been able to make as much as 4.95 points on their reverse mortgages. Also, if you have, or are willing to get, your life insurance license, after the reverse mortgage has funded, you can return to these very same borrowers and offer them suitable insurance products, some of which offer up to an additional ten points in insurance commissions!

You can get paid in a number of ways off of reverse mortgages. The reverse mortgage field is something that a lot of *lenders* are going into, but a lot of *brokers* and loan officers are ignoring. These brokers and LOs mistakenly believe that, "you can only make a couple hundred dollars on a reverse mortgage." That's just not true. There are ways to get nearly 5 points from reverse mortgage lenders who will allow you to charge nearly 5 points on these transactions. Even if you're a loan officer there are ways to get those 5 points and to keep 100 percent of those points! So, if you do things my way, your broker will pass along the whole 5 points to you!

Other opportunities in this current mortgage market are things like the FHA Streamline refinance. In many of these cases you don't even need a new appraisal, just new income documentation to verify that they're still working. And still another opportunity in this market is for Fannie/Freddie ARM resets, prime mortgage borrowers whose adjustable rate mortgages are resetting. These borrowers had good credit but they refinanced for the lowest interest rate possible, on an adjustable rate mortgage. Then they went out and bought more and more stuff: cars, motorcycles, splurges at Best Buy, who knows what else, leaving them with no disposable income left to work with. When their adjustable rate mortgages adjust on them, they need to refinance into either a new ARM or into a fixed rate mortgage. These people come to my members through the marketing that I create for my members, and soon they're paying my members between 5 and 7.99 points, depending on whether or not your state has a fee cap lower than the federal caps of 7.99 points and 10 points (8 to 10 points is Section 32). Even though these were prime borrowers, they will happily pay the maximum legal fee in your state!

The media has caused quite a scare in the mortgage market by painting things with too broad a brush.

They've given the impression that none of the mortgages currently out there are going to be repaid, which is foolish. The media does stuff like that. When they talk about foreclosures, they count all legal filings as foreclosures, when in fact, not every foreclosure filing is an actual foreclosure. We know that when people fall 90 days behind on their mortgage, there's a Notice of Default ("NOD") filed at the county courthouse. The media counts that—every legal filing, all the way through the foreclosure process, which could take a year in many cases. They even count the foreclosure redemption notice when the borrower catches up by either refinancing or paying off the past-due amount! The media really does everyone a disservice because they are in the business of *selling* news, and the news that is most saleable, gets the most attention, i.e.: the scary stuff. The media should always be treated with distrust and skepticism.

The role that government has played in the current mortgage market has been one of deregulation over the last 20 to 30 years, and I think this is a good thing because it has provided more people with the ability to own their own homes. Some would say that certain Americans shouldn't have that ability; I don't believe that at all. I think that every American should have the ability to try their hand at they've homeownership, and that they should accept the risks and the rewards that come with it. People need the chance to accept personal responsibility by making mortgage payments that they've promised to make. I don't see anything wrong with an adjustable rate mortgage, and I don't see anything wrong with refinancing from one adjustable rate mortgage to another adjustable rate. I totally reject the idea that more government is better; instead, it seems like everything the government gets involved in they screw up. If you look at everything from how much a bolt on the space shuttle costs to what we pay for hammers and toilet seats for the Department of Defense, you'll see that proper money management and government don't go hand-in-hand. I think we should trust individuals and free financial markets to work things out themselves.

When it comes to big business's role in our current mortgage situation, there are several for us to discuss. With the creation of Fannie Mae and Freddie Mac, a secondary market was created, so that mortgages could be moved off of the books of small local banks. Well, small neighborhood banks are terrible at the mortgage process because they view themselves as bankers, not as people who solve problems for homeowners, nor as folks who enable homeownership. The "big players," such as Washington Mutual or Ditech (which is owned by GMAC) don't do a very good job at serving people in the local market. That creates a huge opportunity for the local mortgage broker or LO to provide great personalized service and a face-to-face experience that people just can't get from the big impersonal mortgage lenders.

In the mortgage market and in the housing market, every few years, there's a boom and a bust. What's happening right now isn't exceptional; it's happened before, and it'll happen again. Warren Buffett says, "When other people are greedy, be scared; and when they are scared, be greedy." So, my excitement about the current mortgage market is that this is a terrific time to seize market share—not that you should do a million transactions, but there are a whole bunch of loan officers and brokers who have left the business, and who have left their past borrowers ready to be picked off!

The mortgage market is cyclical, but that doesn't mean that your income needs to be.

Look at it this way. In a boom, there's a whole flood of people that come into the business off of the car lots or from selling vacuums. So what you need in boom times is a mortgage marketing system that sets you apart. Then, you can get those big fees and have no rate or fee resistance from your borrowers.

Now, in a refi "bust," a whole bunch of people leave the business, but there's also a lot less business to do, so you definitely need a mortgage marketing system. The important thing is to de-commoditize yourself so that folks don't think of you as the mortgage guy. If you can do this, then you'll have no rate or fee resistance, and you'll be able to eat through the winter. In fact, you'll be able to seize market share, and do nearly as well as you did in the boom. In the "down market" of 2008, the folks still using my system have still had a very good year, in spite of current market conditions. It's a system that collects all sorts of business in the wake of all the people who have walked off the battlefield and gone into insurance and multi-level marketing, or back to wherever they came from.

No matter how unusual it sounds, no matter how much this flies in the face of what is commonly accepted as the "industry norm," with a mortgage marketing system, you can do nearly as well in a refi bust as you did in the refi boom.

The people who use my system utilize my Tucker Past Borrower Retention System® for their own past borrowers so that they can keep in constant contact—not in a manner that would cause them to be viewed as "the mortgage guy," but just kind of keeping in touch through automated means that seem very, very personal. Talk to your past borrowers as if they're friends, not as if they're past customers!

Now what we do in times when other people are leaving the mortgage business is we create what our emotional direct response marketing systems, such as the Tucker Reverse Mortgage Marketing System®, or the Tucker Fannie/Freddie Prime ARM Reset System®, or the Tucker FHA Refi System®, and we take in these new borrowers, who used to be somebody else's, in the "front door" of our mortgage marketing funnel, and after their loan funds, they have become *ours*. We have seized someone else's past borrower(s), as that broker or LO has either left the business, or done a bad job of retaining their past borrowers. Now we plug them into the Tucker Past Borrower Retention System®. So this is a big part of how we profit wildly from a "down market."

So we have real estate prices climb for a period of, say a decade, and then we have them decline for maybe 2 or 3 years, and then climb again for another decade or so, and the cycle goes on and on. We also have a similar cycle that happens with interest rates, where interest rates rise over time, and then they are cut, and they go back up, and they're cut again. Most people in and out of the mortgage business think that you have to starve if you choose to stay in the business in a "down market." Well, that's dead wrong, as I've just explained to you. Please always keep in mind that contrarians win very, very big in business and in life. You've got to do your own thinking, not let quitters and poor-performers tell you what you should settle for. It's very possible that with a mortgage system that's well thought out—one that is adapted and targeted for a changed mortgage market—that you can earn *more* in a "down market" than you did in a "good" market, while in the good market, you operated without a proper mortgage marketing system.

What you should learn from the past decade of lending is that lending standards are *also* cyclical, so underwriting criteria loosens as all the lenders fight over business in boom times. We've seen this before as well; it's nothing new. In the late 1990s and early 2000s, we were in a long cycle of loosening lending standards, and now we're in a cycle of tightening them. Well, this will not last. We'll go back into a position where the lenders all decide that they should be lending more aggressively, which is of course what they ought to be doing right now, because they've overcorrected. When they decide that they all ought to be lending, they're going to go back out there, rate sheets and guidelines in hand, and they're going to come at you with a bucketful of money. There's a lot of cash on the sidelines right now from investors and they're going to begin to see mortgages in a new light, and they're going to loosen their underwriting standards, and hand out bucketsful of cash all over again. But what I want to get across to you is that you can make money in *any* mortgage market, once you have a firm grasp of how to properly use a mortgage marketing system in *both* kinds of markets!

In loosening cycles, some lenders make loans seemingly just so that they can put-up big quarterly volume numbers in the trade magazines, never mind loan quality. It's investors chasing returns that really caused the current mess we're in, because they made loans they shouldn't have. They were making money no matter whom they leant to—but that can only last for so long. And as Will Rogers said, "I'm more concerned with the return *of* my money, than the return *on* my money." That's the attitude all investors should have, instead of investing their entire portfolio in mortgage-backed securities they don't understand.

The 80/20 Rule

I'm a big believer in the 80/20 rule, also known as the Pareto principle. What the 80/20 rule says as it pertains to the mortgage business is that 80% of the money in the business is made by only 20% of the people; and, of course, 20% of people are making 80% of the money. This is important to be aware of because it means that if 10 mortgage brokers are asked how the business is going, 8 of them will say, "Man, it's a hard business. I can't make any money in this market; all the borrowers care about is rate and fee." And those eight out of 10 brokers will form the average person's opinion of how the mortgage business is going.

But the reality is that 2 out of 10 mortgage brokers are making all the money, and they're doing so because they have a reliable mortgage marketing system. They're not relying on chasing realtors with boxes of donuts and rate sheets; they're not relying on slashing fees, nor bait-and-switch. They are busily *marketing*, and as a result of that marketing, they're working less, but making more, because their borrowers behave the way borrowers *should* behave. Their borrowers, gained through their marketing, are attracted to them, not repulsed. The borrowers are *not* asking them to cut rates and they're not asking them to cut fees. The twenty percent guys are cleaning up, and *those* are the guys that everybody wants to be like! For some reason, the other 80% never asks them for their secret.

Instead, people in the mortgage business usually emulate the habits and tactics of the *unsuccessful* broker, not of the successful one. They do this because they focus upon the majority...the 8 out of 10 brokers that they see doing things "the way everyone else in this business does them." They never take the time to understand how the *successful* mortgage broker became successful. Maybe it's hard to pick the successful ones out of the crowd, as this business is full of flashy pretenders. By successful, I mean not working 80-hour weeks. If you're making $100,000.00 a year but working 80 hours a week, I don't consider you to be a success. Certainly you cannot be considered a success with your family, just for starters.

Understand that anything you do more than once should be systematized.

If you find yourself doing the same things over and over again, by brawn and grunt work, then you desperately need to rethink things, and develop systems for everything you do more than once. To me, success is making $500,000.00 a year while working 20 hours a week. That's successful in my eyes because it means you're a success with your family, with your friends, and with yourself, not just with customers or bank tellers. You got into this business so that your business would reward you financially, so that you could live a rich life, and so that your business would serve you, not so you could serve your business, at all waking hours, and even at hours at which you should be sleeping!

The 80/20 rule also says that of those top 20% of mortgage brokers, that that group again divides itself into *another* 80/20 scenario, in which the top 20% of the top 20% are also making more than the remainder of that original top 20%! When you apply the 80/20 rule to a mortgage brokerage, it says that you need not serve all 10 borrowers in the marketplace. You need only serve 2 out of 10! So really, what you *should* be doing is creating a niche for your mortgage business, not going "broad" and acting as a generalist. There should be loan types you focus on and borrowers you focus upon because otherwise you're just spitting in the ocean. Your mortgage marketing dollars are so diffused and diluted on so many people that you have no meaningful affect on anybody.

My system is designed to put you in that top 20% of the top 20%. There are three niches that are of great opportunity right now. One is reverse mortgages, another is FHA Streamline refi's, and another is Fannie/Freddie prime ARM resets. Focus in on any one of these categories, or even all three, and you can make an absolute killing in today's market. So the idea that you should serve everybody, the sort of Wal-Mart philosophy that it's always low prices and everybody's welcome, is wrong. No, not all customers are good customers, not all customers are profitable customers; and if you err on the side of high fees, charging the legal maximum on every deal—which is made possible by good mortgage marketing—then you'll always be okay in the mortgage business because you'll always have a high net income.

When you get into the game of cutting prices, please remember that you're not lending your own money, so you can't afford to cut your fees. Sure, Ditech can do it for lower rates and no fees because they're lending their own money. Plus, they've cut out the expense of maintaining a local retail office. You, however, have to charge for your service, because you do not make any interest on the money lent.

The way you should apply the 80/20 rule is to look at everyone around you and decide who the successful 20-percenters are. Look for somebody that has that sort of thing, somebody who has a system, not somebody who just pedals faster. Pedaling faster will exhaust you and you will have no quality of life. Your spouse will divorce you and take half your assets anyway. So what you should be doing is figuring out who the successful 20-percenters are and then figure out who has the best *lifestyle* of all of them. You will soon come to the conclusion that people in the top 20% have good *lifestyles* and don't work their tails off every week. These people have a system for *everything*.

The Time Is Now

There's never a "bad time" to enter the mortgage business. Most people think that they have to wait for the next big wave, as if this were surfing. I think *both* times are good times to enter. If you enter during a refi boom, it's a good time to enter because there's lots of business and the market's very forgiving of newbies. But like I said, there's no reason to wait for a refi boom. A good time to get in the mortgage business is also in "tough times" because there's been a huge vacuum created by people exiting the business. Why? Because they weren't good salespeople and they didn't market themselves directly to borrowers effectively. If you're a good marketer and a decent salesperson who has the support of a mortgage marketing system, then you'll find that a whole bunch of the noise and chatter has left; you with your mortgage marketing system will be able to plug in and do just as well as you would in a refi boom!

For the mortgage broker or loan officer starting out or looking to grow, opportunities abound to learn how to create a mortgage marketing system for yourself, and how to plug that into your business. Really, the only limitations you have are those you impose upon yourself. You know, Santa Claus doesn't do it to you, the Devil doesn't do it to you, and the government doesn't do it to you. Your outcomes are determined by your own state of mind and what *you* believe is possible. If you read a book a week on direct response marketing and apply what you've learned, if you'll do just one thing each day to move yourself in a positive direction towards your goals, you'll arrive at your destination. Consistency is more important than spurts of activity.

It's sort of like exercise. Not exercising all year and then making a New Year's resolution come January 1 that you'll spend two hours a day at the gym and eat rice cakes pretty much guarantees that you'll last for about two weeks before you're back to your 50 weeks of neglect, waiting for the next 2-week cycle on the next January 1st. That sort of spurt of activity is far less effective than simply taking a walk every morning for 20 minutes around your neighborhood, but doing it for 50 weeks instead of 2.

So the key is consistency in your own marketing self-education. There are plenty of books on marketing. Don't just study books on mortgage marketing but also books on marketing in general, and emotional direct response marketing specifically; you can read David Ogilvy books and all sorts of things. Just educate yourself bit by bit; it's the same way you eat a cow, one hamburger at a time.

There are always going to be people on the "speakers' circuit" that show up at all the big mortgage trade shows saying that they've been in the business 20 years and that the only thing that you can do is to chase realtors. This is silly.

Realtors are generally a bad source of deals because they get jealous whenever you make as much as they do! They wonder, "who are you to come along to get 5 or 7.99 points on this deal?" Why should you make as much as a realtor? In fact, you should make as much or more than a realtor because *you* are highly skilled, *you* actually provide financing! Remember, they don't just hand out houses without money in return! And *you* can get the deal done, not just shake hands, smile, and talk about getting it done. It's one thing to do open houses; it's quite another to figure out how to finance the deal!

Realtors are also a bad source of deals because usually there are 2 of them. What's worse than one realtor? Two of 'em! And then there are 2 sets of borrowers, usually a husband and a wife, and often a lawyer on each side. So you've got eight people to try to control, and since you got the deal from a realtor in the first place, and since you came into the deal last, you're *never* in control of the deal! And that's just nuts, because that's where your grocery money is supposed to come from! And since buyers' realtor came to you viewing you as a simple commodity...something that they could get for no points any old place, they have zero respect for you. They will try to carve up your fees—but so are the buyers, because they don't want to put any more money into this deal. And don't even get me started on what the lawyers are going to do! They make even less than *realtors,* and man are they pissed about that! "I went through 7 years of post-secondary education, and even passed the bar!" Yeah, well I passed the bar on my way to the bathroom.

So that's yet another one of the dangers of following "conventional wisdom," that "you get deals from realtors." My Tucker Mortgage Marketing System® proves that the *best* way to get deals is to create the leads for yourself! Not to buy them, but to rent mailing lists of existing homeowners, not buyers, and to market to these borrowers to create your own *refi* leads that you own and control, and that no one else has access to!

Summary:

- Reverse mortgages are a very hot opportunity right now, due to FHA-backing, an aging U.S. population, and no income and credit underwriting.
- The real estate market is cyclical, but your income doesn't need to be.
- Most in the mortgage business are failing, so you must learn what you should be doing from the successful few.
- You're not lending your own money, so you have to charge for your time. You can't stay in business charging low fees.
- There's never a bad time to enter the mortgage business.
- Realtors are a poor source of business.

| A | MORTGAGE BROKERAGE NEWS | November 2007 |

"How a bed-ridden Maryland mortgage broker effortlessly raked-in $48,291.33 in fees! Without leaving his hospital bed!"

In 'the worst month ever!' Of the so-called 'mortgage meltdown!'

Clarksville, Maryland-- With the credit markets undergoing a "meltdown," banks in the United Kingdom collapsing under $5 BILLION "runs", the Fed & the European Central Bank pumping in HUNDREDS OF BILLIONS of dollars to shore-up "catastrophically weak" economies, all the panic & hysteria of the so-called "credit crunch" has not prevented 1 mortgage broker from leveraging the secret knowledge of outspoken & unconventional consumer advocate & sub-prime mortgage industry veteran & expert, Scott Tucker.

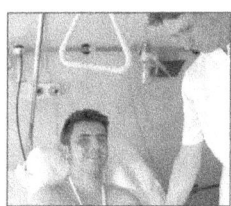

> "They say this was the 'worst month ever' ...but I closed 6 loans...and made $48,291.33 in fee income...from my hospital bed!"

One of Tucker's "MasterMind Members," Kevin Marks, of Clarksville, Maryland, just pumped $48,291.33 in fee income into his bank account, in what most are calling the "dead" market! All while laid-up in his hospital bed!

Marks said, "even while I was laid-up, flat on my back in a hospital bed, Tucker's System kept pulling in borrowers in on auto-pilot! Even though the sub-prime market is supposedly 'dead!'"

"They say this was the 'worst month ever'...but I closed 6 loans...and made $48,291.33 in fee income...from my hospital bed! Here's what happened." Marks con-

was a $380,000.00 refi for 4 points and $15,200.00 in fee income. I had my wife bring in my laptop and my 'lender Bible' into the hospital and it went like clockwork! Smooth as silk! The borrowers came to the hospital to sign the documents! None of this would have happened without Scott Tucker's Past Borrower Retention System!"

2. "A borrower I had set up with a 2/28 'first-step loan' needed to get out of it before it adjusted to a higher rate. He called me a dozen times to get me to help him. Result: a $183,000.00 refi with 4 points in fees! That's $7,400.00 dollars! He too came to the hospital to sign the documents! This would not have happened without Scott Tucker's Past Borrower Retention System!"

3. "A Realtor® who'd seen my Scott Tucker Advertising repeatedly called & faxed my office saying that she just had to talk to me! My wife was bringing my office faxes to the hospital! Turns-out the Realtor® had a couple properties she couldn't refinance because they had 'ground rent.' I made some calls and fixed it for her! Result: $147,234.00 refi at 4.20 points and $6,183.83 in fees, plus a $208,300.00 purchase at 2.5 points and another $5,212.50 in fees! This was all due to the 'guru' status that Scott Tucker's mar-

They were desperate to get that money to tide them over during this 'tough time' in the real estate market. She'd heard I used Scott Tucker's proprietary Members Only website to handle 'hard-to-place loans!' So she called me...and I fixed it for her! Result: 2 investor purchase deals for $285,900 at 2.5 points and another $14,295.00 in fees!"

"That's how Scott Tucker's Program effortlessly generated $48,291.33 in fee income for me while I was flat on my back in my hospital bed!"

Scott Tucker himself is bullish about the current "crisis" and says, "Crisis? All the 'doom & gloom' is media hype. In spite of the current loss of available credit from lenders, borrowers can still get financing through the very same mortgage loan officers they've always relied upon! Via FHA loans!"

"This whole 'credit crunch' is nothing more than a temporary glitch. Lending is not going away, long-term. Sub-prime mortgages are seeing a 4% 'delinquency' rate this year versus the normal & customary 4% 'delinquency' rate!" says Tucker.

"The 'delinquency' rate is not the same as the much lower 'foreclosure' rate. 'Delinquent' borrowers are just late & slow-payers. Most of these borrowers catch-back-up and fall-behind again. Over-and-over again. It's just their habit to do so. The same way some other people might have some other odd habit. The great majority of those 4% who are 'delinquent' do not go into foreclosure. The media act as if 64-million Americans suddenly turned in their house keys. They have not!" Tucker continues.

Tucker concludes, "in the 'worst ever' month, my Member, Kevin Marks, just did $48,291.33 in fees from his hospital bed! Using nothing more than the Secrets I share with everyone who uses my System! Any

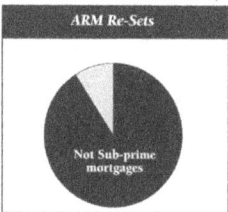

Chapter Two
Widget Wars

Most people view mortgages as something that you can just get from the hardware store. They think one size fits all. They get their information from *USA Today*, which of course fails to take into account credit scores or income documentation of the borrower, or even if this a conventional or a jumbo loan. Is this an FHA or VA loan? Or is it a non-government loan? *USA Today* just quotes you a rate, without asking any questions. So the consumer, when left to these sorts of incomplete yet convincing charts, is encouraged to believe that mortgages are commodities—which is exactly the reason why you should never advertise as a "mortgage guy."

People who believe they only need any old mortgage or refinance have no reason to call you for help because they can just call Ditech or go to Washington Mutual, or Countrywide, or who knows where. If you're just a guy giving them "a mortgage," they're going to treat you like a commodity, because to them, a mortgage is a commodity. When you advertise your rates and fees as if you were running a gas station, you shouldn't be surprised that you attract cheap "price buyers," "tire kickers," and shoppers.

No, the *best* way to market your mortgage business is *not* to market it as a mortgage business at all. Sure, you want to market to homeowners who need your services, but you want to approach them about their existing problems and agitations, their emotions, and the solutions that you can provide as a financial guru. You want to keep the whole "mortgage" conversation out of it. Remember, you are a solution provider, not a "mortgage guy."

When homeowners come to you with their list of problems, I recommend that you keep it a bit "murky" as to exactly how you'll fix everything, until you actually get them to a face-to-face meeting, at your office, where you'll have them sign the disclosures. It will become apparent to them then, that this is, in fact, a mortgage—but you shouldn't put that right out there right at the get-go. Because, who can blame 'em, if you say "mortgage" too early, they see you as just another "mortgage guy," and they discount in their minds the value of all it is that you do for folks with their problems. They should be eased into the mortgage transaction because, let's face it, nobody gets excited about having "a shiny new mortgage!" "Hey Gladys, it's got that 'new mortgage' smell!" What they get excited about is problems solved, emotions at ease, being able to sleep at night, and finding a way to afford the kids' Catholic school tuition. They don't care about a *mortgage*. They care about *themselves* and what's in it for *them*. So keep in mind what's in it for *them*, and stop marketing to them with "a mortgage message." You really have no place in the mortgage business if all you do is provide a mortgage; homeowners can get *that* anywhere.

Now, a mortgage has the potential to solve any number of problems, including those that may have been created by an old, "outdated" mortgage. A mortgage can solve the problems that a car lease or auto loan has created. It can solve the problems that filing for bankruptcy cannot solve, and/or that credit counseling cannot solve. It can solve the problems of their maxed-out credit cards, and their high and non-tax-deductable interest can create.

When you present a mortgage as a tool that can be used by you, the financial guru, to solve all their problems, rather than just presenting it as a "mortgage refinance,"

> you have the ability to put any legal fee
> on it that you wish, and so, I suggest that
> you ask for the maximum legal fee in your
> jurisdiction.

Usually 5 to 7.99 points. Please remember that so-called "prime" borrowers have all the same problems that non-prime borrowers have. Just because somebody has a 780 credit score rather than a 580 doesn't change anything. They're not any less troubled by their problems. They don't necessarily make any more money; they just have a better credit score, which means they're a bit of a better risk for the lender. But you as a broker are going to do as much work with them as you would with any other borrower, so you need to charge the maximum legal fee. You don't do anyone any favors by cutting fees and going out of business. If they don't like it, let them go somewhere else; but they can't take up any more of your time. Remember, your mortgage marketing system creates as many borrowers as you'll ever need, but you can't spend time with borrowers who don't want to pay for it.

The only thing you have to sell is your time, and you can only do so many deals a month. I say to keep it to five deals a month anyway, just do the maximum legal fee on each of them. If you give away a week's worth of time to a borrower only paying 1 point instead of to a borrower paying 5 or 7.99 points, then you've cheated yourself terribly—and you've probably *lost* money doing that loan for one point versus not doing it at all!

In my mind, brokers, and everybody else in business life, are middlemen; it's not for brokers to tell people they can't take out a loan that they qualify for. No more than it is for a car dealer to tell someone, "You're a lousy driver!" It's not within a broker's control to keep a borrower from taking out a loan, nor is it within a broker's control to keep an investor from buying a mortgage-backed security. The mortgage broker really is somebody who is supposed to facilitate the origination process at a local, retail level; and the mortgage broker has to do that legally, ethically, and morally, making sure there's no fraud in the file. It's really not the mortgage broker's place to get in the way of consumer choice.

The idea that there are winners and losers in commerce, I think, is a completely false one. It's the sort of thinking that Karl Marx might come up with. In commerce, there's never any such thing as a loser. There are people who benefit in different ways and different parts of the transaction. So, if I sell you something for $5,000.00, you haven't lost the money, you've gained a thing of value that is worth $5,000.00, or *more*, in *your* eyes. We've each agreed that the thing we got from the other is *better* than the thing we gave up. And for that reason, no one *ever* loses in commerce. I don't care what Dan Rather says!

Remember the 80/20 rule—that 80% of Americans are making the 20% of the money and 20% of that group are making the majority of the money in the first 20% group; and of that 20%, 20% of them are making 80% of the money in the first top 20% group. Eighty percent of Americans, that CNN's Lou Dobbs might call "those less fortunate" oftentimes have *decided* to be less fortunate. When you're a child, your parents' low income is not your fault. But when you're an adult, your income *is* your responsibility.

I think we follow the conventional wisdom of how business "should be done," just because "it's the way everybody else does it." Certainly every opportunity you have to de-commoditize the mortgage process, and to do the entire process *differently*, while of course still 100% legally, should be investigated. It's the Walt Disney idea—he said his theme parks should be *different* from every other theme park. I'll even say that you should run your mortgage brokerage as a theme park of sorts. You should make doing business with you fun and exciting for your borrowers, and you should really be thinking "outside the box" as they say. Whenever a borrower comes to your office for a scheduled application or a scheduled closing, they should have the theme park experience—have a juke box in your office, a Coke machine that gives out free soda, a model train that runs around up by the ceiling, model airplanes, sports memorabilia, you name it. Have all kinds of crazy stuff in your office, so that it feels like one of Walt's theme parks, a *fun* experience that people look forward to getting more of, not a boring institution, such as a bank! Don't make a trip to your office like a trip to the dentist!

In my office waiting area, there are a couple of fold-down chairs from Wrigley Field that they tore out during a reconstruction in the 1990s, and at the foot of the chairs are foot massagers. Borrowers are invited to take their shoes off and get a little massage, and while they're doing this they watch a repeating DVD on the waiting area flat screen TV, of what appears to be a real broadcast of a TV show, that sort of looks like an infomercial, but that features me, a fake TV host, and my real past borrowers, interviewed in their homes.

Decorating the room are a bunch of Navy and Marine Corps model airplanes and helicopters, and a replica of the U.S.S. Theodore Roosevelt (CVN 71), which was the aircraft carrier I was on in the Navy. Also on display are my Navy medals, my dad's Navy medals, and my grandpa's Army Air Corps medals. This gives borrowers an idea of who I am and what makes me tick.

There's also an old Wurlitzer jukebox in the office. Frequently, Boomer or Stinky, my chocolate Labradors, will greet the people when they come in; the dogs are an especially big hit when people bring in their kids at their appointments. In the conference room, I have a Chicago Bears-themed vending machine that dispenses cans of soda, bottled water, and even cans of beer, without depositing any coins! Most guys, right around 5 p.m. or so, can't resist asking, "Hey, you got beer in there!?" And I say, "Yup, we've got beer in here, and it's free. You don't need any quarters or anything. And if you want, I'll have a beer with you. Just go ahead and push that button. Just don't get all drunk on me, okay?"

Of course, I'm not saying that you or your borrower should be *intoxicated* when signing disclosures, but one beer isn't going to do that to a beer drinker. You just want to make your borrowers feel at home when they come to meet with you. And if you've got a nice cold beer for them after work, it really makes them feel like you're just one of the guys, and that you're not just after them for their money.

Also, the chairs that we sit on in the conference room are some very nice ones with massager in them. The restroom offers a fancy heated Toto brand toilet seats (that also cleans you if you like), and another TV that plays the very same "fake TV show" that they saw in the waiting area. Oh, and I should mention, that every part of the office has those heated oil air fresheners, which the ladies (and even I) really like.

In the conference area where we meet is the same "fake TV show" DVD recording set to repeat. So, in every sense that they have that I can "manipulate," I manipulate. Just as ol' Walt would do at his theme parks! Did you know that under the tables of one of Walt's theme park restaurants, they put little speakers under the tables that make frog noises? Whether at Walt's, or in my office, no detail is too small to pay attention to, and to plan for. The important word in all of this is "plan."

I have the whole office *choreographed*.
Use *every* sense they've got: sight, sound,
scent, how things in the office feel...

(remember the heated toilet seat?), and even the taste of a cold beverage! You need to immerse the borrower in your fun, exciting, and *enjoyable* "theme park" experience. Bubba, this is how you get referrals and repeat business! Not by some lame cookie cutter interest rate decrease notice!

So many brokers have the idea that we are actually in "competition" with other mortgage brokers—but members of my system are not. If you're a problem solver, not a "mortgage broker," then you're no longer in competition with other mortgage brokers, and you don't need to be in the mindset of cutting fees and interest rates to compete. You don't need to use those weak tactics because that's not *your* business; it's not even the same game. You need to have a mortgage marketing system that treats the borrower as someone who has problems that you're able to solve, and you need to apply a lot of empathy. Put yourself in the borrower's shoes. Ask them a lot of non-mortgage questions. Ask, "And how does that make you feel? I bet it kinda frustrates you, huh?" You can succeed by *not* competing in a head-to-head commodity war with other brokers. And when you do this, you're able to sell at rates and fees *higher* than your "competitors!"

And, you'll find it's incredibly easy, especially when you've *planned* the whole process, rather than just fumbling through it. For instance, don't like the borrowers you're attracting? Use different bait! *Plan* everything to be *different* from every other broker in your area, and start with the *marketing*. But work all the way through the *entire* process, including past borrower retention!

This probably seems counterintuitive to you because most mortgage brokers and loan officers get into the business thinking they should learn from their peers. Well, this is like having clueless parents and learning bad behaviors from them. Doesn't make much sense, does it? Who they *should* be learning from, when it comes to mortgage marketing, are the most successful guys in the business—the top 20% of the top 20%—the guys who make the *most* while working the *least*. Anything that anybody *else* does is really something to be ignored and even shunned. The top 20% make their money while living the greatest *lifestyle* possible, which includes a marketing system, and layers of automation, that allow them to free up their time! I think you'll find that the things the most successful men and women in this business have in common are that they emulate *only* the *successful* brokers, and that they also *think* for themselves. They don't get *marketing* advice, from a silly continuing ed. instructor who's really there only to teach them about the Truth-in-Lending Act. And they don't take in any new mortgage marketing information without challenging it, and without asking "Why?" Or, "Is that the *best* way to do that?"

Summary:

- The best way to market a mortgage is not to talk about the mortgage at all.
- Your borrowers don't "lose" because you charge a high fee. Rather, they benefit from greater attention from you as a result.
- Your office should be an escape from the normal, day-to-day, dreary experience your borrower has outside your office.
- Make sure your marketing, and your office, tells your "biography" in an interesting way.
- Use "props" in your office that further strengthen the sale that you've already made over the phone, and from your printed marketing.
- Cater to every sense your borrowers have to make them completely comfortable in your office.
- Plan every step of the sales process, before the sale needs to be made.

PERSONAL FINANCE | BY RACHEL RICHARDS

HOMEOWNERS IN TROUBLE TURN TO 'HOME LOAN INSIDER' FOR THE TRUTH ABOUT MONEY!

"Face it: Your creditors have intentionally set you up to fail, and are profiting from your hardship!"

HAVE YOU EVER thought about how crazy it is that just when you can't afford to make your payments on time, your creditors charge you even more money? If you had the money you owed them, you wouldn't be paying late in the first place!

WHEN BAD THINGS HAPPEN TO GOOD PEOPLE!

Find yourself coming up short every month? "Coming up short" means more late fees, and even more penalties! And that just keeps the cycle going!

IT'S NOT YOUR FAULT IF YOU'VE HAD CREDIT PROBLEMS.

Your creditors want to keep you in the dark on purpose! Scott Tucker knows for a fact that they want you in the dark! And he wants to show everyday, hard-working, Chicago-area homeowners the light!

Scott has helped hundreds of homeowners just like you. So what can Scott do about your problems? In his own words, "I spend every waking moment socking it to today's 'credit bullies,' 'fat cat bankers,' and 'predatory lenders!'"

Scott has been where you are now, and he knows exactly why and how homeowners and their families are being put at an unfair disadvantage! Better yet, Scott knows how to fix it! Forever!

He learned all his secrets from the inside of the very industry he now rails against! Rather than perpetuating their abuse, he NOW works hard for neighborhood families and their financial turnarounds! He's been offered plenty of jobs at all the "big banks," and understandably so!

This reporter recommends that you call Scott immediately so you won't ever have to be in this depressing hole of debt ever again!

You're so busy trying to make your ridiculous minimum monthly payments, that you don't have any time at all available to spend learning the ins, outs, and secrets of the very system that holds you down!

He can repair your credit for you, while you watch TV! He knows how to go about cleaning it up and boosting your damaged credit score almost instantly. Learn the truth about "credit counseling." Why is the Federal Trade Commission shutting those scamsters down?

He'll wipe out all your credit card balances, without filing for a bankruptcy! He can get you better interest rates, and show you how to legally, morally, and ethically write-off 100% of the interest you pay! Just like the "fat cats" do!

Even consumers with no credit at all can access more financial opportunities, thanks to Scott Tucker!

Could you handle getting 2 months no bills to pay? No mortgage? No car notes? No credit cards?

"I'll save you hundreds to thousands of dollars every month! Money you now throw down the toilet!" Scott says. "And not only that, but you'll live better than you do now! This is no 'coupon-clipping' type of thing!"

Is this guy for real? He claims he can get you as much as $200,000.00 in CASH! While still saving you money each month! "I've even gotten folks more than that in the past," he brags! "Some only want $10,000 in cash! Or none at all! Hey, it's your choice! Just tell me which way you want it!" Tucker says.

All his claims are outrageous! And sound too good to be true! Until he showed me proof in the form of written, audio, and even video testimonials! Credit reports before and after! Even checks and disbursement statements!

The truth is, you're in trouble right now—it will make zero difference to him whether you choose to ask him for help or not. But we both know it will make a tremendous difference to you if you don't!

HOME LOAN TRAPS

Scott Tucker revealed to me home loan traps that "they" hope you don't find out about!

HOME LOAN TRAP #1: NEGATIVE AMORTIZATION

A few years back, Scott learned about "negative amortization," a dirty little secret of many home loans! Basically, negative amortization is a fancy name for a lender giving you a loan where each month, your monthly payment not only does NOT pay down your principal balance—but it does NOT even pay for all of the interest you owe for that month!

With a "negative amortization" loan, your

continued on page 32

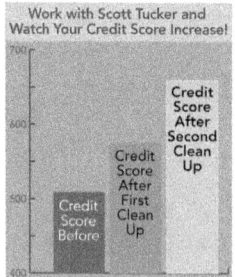
Scott Tucker and loyal friend Boomer

Work with Scott Tucker and Watch Your Credit Score Increase!

Credit Score Before

Credit Score After First Clean Up

Credit Score After Second Clean Up

Source: fromdebttosavings.com

Chapter Three
Emotional Connection

Nothing is sold logically. Most people don't realize this; they'll say they bought a car because it gets the best gas mileage, or because the old one was acting up. But they really bought the new car because they were *emotionally* excited about the vehicle, not because it was "practical." There are folks that regularly buy $50,000.00 automobiles when they could buy $10,000 ones.

If you think that things are sold logically or based upon price, just ask yourself, "Am I driving the cheapest car I could find? Am I wearing the cheapest shirt I could buy? Am I eating the cheapest food I could find? Am I living in the cheapest house or apartment I can afford?" You'll answer no to all these questions if you're really honest with yourself, and you'll confess that you too buy things *emotionally* the same way everybody else does. Of course, after you've had your emotions play games with your wallet, you'll tell your friends, "Hey, I'm no fool. I bought this car because it gets good gas mileage, has a 5-star safety rating, and my old car was probably going to break down any day now." You'll tell them you're not subject to the very same buying emotions that everyone is subject to. "I bought this car because it makes logical sense." Phooey! The facts of human buying behavior say otherwise!

The Pain Factor

Everybody has pain in some area, and with mailing lists we can reach only and exactly the people who have a predetermined assortment of pains—via public county courthouse records, U.S. Bankruptcy Court records, modeled data, self-reported consumer data, TiVo® viewer behavioral data, automobile ownership data, warranty card collected information, whatever. The variety of sources is endless. We can send a mail piece to a prospective borrower who has a known emotional pain, or who is very likely to have that emotional pain, and market to them with our problem-solving formula, identifying their specific problem(s). Your job is to hit their emotional hot buttons, "agitating" them, and get them all worked up about it. And then you present yourself, not "a mortgage refinance," as the solution to their assortment of problems, emotional pains, agitations, anxieties, etcetera.

Don't present the "mortgage refinance" as the solution; present *yourself* as the solution. Because there are a million places they can get a mortgage, but there's only one of you. And, they don't know how much you are "supposed to cost." When you do this, they forget to ask about rate and fee, even though they happily sign all your disclosures, fully disclosing to them that you charge the maximum legal fee in your jurisdiction. You are now the guru, no longer "a mortgage guy." It's only later, when they meet with you at your office, to sign the application paperwork, that they realize that they're getting a new mortgage to solve their problems. The mortgage is just a tool. Don't present it as something they should want, because no one really wants a mortgage, they want solutions and things done for them. Now sure, in states where you're required to disclose in your marketing that you're a mortgage broker, you've done so. But, with proper mortgage marketing that is not focused upon the product (a mortgage refinance), they don't even notice. And, they don't think of you as a "mortgage guy." Even though you did everything 100% legally, you didn't really market them a mortgage refinance. You marketed to them about their known problems and emotions, and then presented yourself as their pain reliever.

To market yourself as their problem-solver, you're going to use information on what's possible for them. You're going to use 24-hour free recorded messages. A website with even more info. Testimonials, and information about you as a person, not as "a mortgage guy," and so on. Always remember, people really don't want to think for themselves; they want things solved for them. We can see this in the masses who believe everything and anything the media tells them, without any critical thought whatsoever. You might dare say we see it in religion. We definitely see it in presidential politics. "Just do it for me." When you fix all their problems for them, presenting them with a slew of benefits, all bundled together, you'll be surprised, I think, at how easily people "go with it." How their defenses go down so effortlessly. Interest rate and fees are no longer of any concern. They even forget to ask all those silly rate and fee questions that Suze Orman told them about, because they no longer care. It's no longer relevant. They've gotten what they really care about—the solution to their financial problems. Finally, they can get a good night's sleep. And remember, this is true of *all* borrowers. Prime or not. Everyone who is about to respond to your properly done mortgage marketing comes to you with problems and anxieties in mind. It's your job to ask what they are! No one buys their groceries with braggadocios stories of how low their mortgage interest rate is. They need their monthly cash flow in order to be able to buy those groceries. That's why what you do for them is so much more important than how low of a rate you give them. In fact, the interest rate is irrelevant.

They really are 100% okay with the idea that they don't know *how* you're doing all this stuff. Actually, this increases your value in their eyes. If they don't tell their friends, "I don't know how he does it!" then you're not doing it right! They'll just go with the flow if you will; later, when they realize that you're doing all this with a mortgage, it does not open you up to any price competition because they're way beyond the "shopping" stage; in fact, they never entered "shopper mode," because you contacted them about problems, not about products! By the time they realize you're doing all this with a mortgage, they're already *past* the commitment stage! They already committed to you long before, and even better yet, theirs was an *emotional* commitment. This emotional commitment is as strong as cement. Even when they find-out that it's "a mortgage," they now don't believe that *anybody* else can do what *you* can do, because from the get-go, you've established yourself as a guru, via your marketing, testimonials, etcetera, and so on. Now everybody *else* in the business presents himselfhimself or herself like a used-car salesman who's trying to push a mortgage on them! And salesmen who "chase" are shunned by consumers. It's just the same as if I were to see you on the street and chase after you. Instinctively, you're gonna run like hell. But see, in the scenario I described above, your properly done marketing has simply only presented them with *information* on what's possible for them in terms of pain relief, benefits, and outcome. And that has caused the prospect to chase *you*, which is what you really want, isn't it? You're damned right it is! *That* is where you get selling power and price-elasticity! To them, you're going to a much deeper level, say ten times as deep, in their minds, making the routine seem miraculous, but really doing a very similar amount of work to what anybody else does. However, you are hitting all of their emotional hot buttons, and taking care of them in a very *empathetic* way, and *that* is something that almost no one else in the mortgage business ever does!

Self-perception is one of the most important things in your entire life, not just in business, but also personally. If you believe that you're a person of value, and by that I mean you have high self-esteem, then you will feel good about yourself, you will do well for others, you will of course be compensated for everything you do in adequate proportion to what you do for others, because you'll have no problem speaking up for yourself and saying, "I deserve 5 points," or "I deserve 7.99

points." However, if you have a low opinion of yourself, you will not try to achieve very much. You will be insecure and therefore snipe with others trying to tear them down to the level at which you perceive yourself to be. Self-image is an extremely important part of your personal *and* business life.

The best way to communicate with your borrowers is in an empathetic fashion. So that they believe that you care more about *them* than about making the sale. Of course, this is never 100% true, as you care about your outcomes and income yourself, but you should always have some sincere caring for your borrowers. And you must go all-out to make sure that this caring comes across to them. Just think of Bill Clinton's "I feel your pain." His empathetic statement, whether real or fake, won him an election to "leader of the free world." Made him, for 8 years, the most powerful man in the world. That's how powerful empathy is in salesmanship. You must make sure that you convey this empathy to them, because if they feel that you're only in it for yourself they will flee. If they believe that you care about them, however, and you're able to take care of all their concerns, they will be loyal to you. And they will have feeling for you. In fact, a very important reason to always charge the maximum legal fee in your jurisdiction is to be able to slow down, do fewer transactions per month, but at greater gross and net profits, and put in more time with each family you help. I believe there is no so-called "predatory fee"; it's whatever the *market* will bear, and if the borrower agrees to it, then it is fully ethical, legal, and moral. Only when you charge them a higher fee, can you give them a higher level of service—*and that's what folks really want.* In fact, most consumers are not cheap. That's a fallacy, as I explained earlier with my questions, "Are <u>you</u> wearing the cheapest shirt you could find?" "Are you driving the cheapest car?"

Most folks in the mortgage business find borrowers by accident, if at all.

Or they try to get them from *other people* who control them, which is a bad way to do things, because that means that these other people also come to control you! Borrowing your power from others puts you in a weak position, not a strong one, and that just sucks. Yet most LOs will go, typically, to a realtor as their number one lead-gathering method; or, they might go to an attorney who handles purchases. Again, the problem with this is that you are putting other people between you and your borrower. This realtor, attorney, whomever, will feel as though they are in control, because the borrower contacted them first. You just came along today. And you came on bended-knee. Salesmen who arrive on bended-knee get their teeth kicked-out. These "lead providers" will feel entitled to pressure you to trim your fees, and will spend the remainder of their time 2nd-guessing everything you do! Doesn't that sound like fun?

These kinds of situations are nightmares and should be avoided at all costs. You should find borrowers *yourself* using a mortgage marketing system that *attracts* borrowers to you that no one else is even talking to. People who don't even know that they want a mortgage, but people who have problems that you can solve with a mortgage refinance.

With all the ways there are nowadays to *automate* your marketing, there really is no reason to screw around with uncooperative realtors or attorneys. There are things nowadays such as 24-hour free recorded messages…it's possible to, with the push of a button, send personalized-sounding voice broadcast messages to your past borrowers, there are tele-seminars and even "evergreen" tele-seminar replays that borrowers *think* are live, there are websites with online video testimonials, audio testimonials, and online application forms. There are 24-hour call centers that will take your inbound phone call leads, all the while appearing to be your very own assistant, in your own office, and they'll run your 20-question application script for you! They then e-mail you the results of each person's 20-question application, so you don't have to talk to anybody. Why work so hard, if you don't have to? There are countless ways to automate not only the acquisition of new borrowers, but also the retention of your past borrowers for repeat transactions and increased referrals.

Summary:

- Nothing is bought logically. Things are only bought emotionally.
- You need a healthy self-esteem to be able to charge high prices.
- Having empathy for your borrowers is essential to making the sale.

Section A	HEALTHY FINANCE NEWS	January 2007

PLANNING STARTS WITH THE BASICS

Jonathan Citrin

When developing a plan for your finances, the toughest question often is: "Where do I begin?" Before investing in stocks and bonds or buying life insurance, before implementing any change or making any decisions, you first need to analyze and understand your entire financial picture.

Two documents allow you to do just that. A Balance Sheet and a Cash Flow Statement enable you to take an in-depth look at your current financial situation and make better decisions about the future.

With a little work, you can develop these two tools and be on your way to a solid plan for your finances.

BALANCE SHEET

A balance sheet is a snapshot of your personal finances at one point in time. It contains two main elements: what you own (assets), and what you owe (liabilities). Your net worth is expressed Net Worth = Assets − Liabilities. That

Lose Weight FAST!
New diet pill melts fat away
1-18-623-5489

what you own minus what you owe. A balance sheet clearly lists all assets and liabilities. Examples of assets include home, investments such as stocks and bonds, savings and checking accounts, 401(k), IRAs, business interests, artwork and jewelry, among others.

Liabilities include mortgage balances, credit cards, education loans, and any other debt. Once you have created a list

Home Owners in Trouble Turn to 'Home Loan Insider' for the Truth About Money!

Rachel Richards – Chicago, IL

Have you ever thought about how crazy it is that just when you can't afford to make your payments on time, your creditors charge you even more money? If you had the money you owed them, you wouldn't be paying late in the first place! Face it. Your creditors have intentionally set you up to fail, and are profiting from your hardship!

WHEN BAD THINGS HAPPEN TO GOOD PEOPLE!

Find yourself coming up short every month? "Coming up short" means more late fees, and even more penalties! And that just keeps the cycle going!

IT'S NOT YOUR FAULT IF YOU'VE HAD CREDIT PROBLEMS.

Your creditors want to keep you in the dark on purpose! Scott Tucker knows for a fact that they want you in the dark! And he wants to show everyday, hard-working Chicago area homeowners the light!

Scott has helped hundreds of homeowners just like you. So what can Scott do about your problems? In his own words: "I spend every waking moment seeking it to today's credit bullies, fat cat bankers, and 'predatory lenders!'"

Scott has been where you are now, and he knows exactly why and how homeowners and their families are being put at an unfair disadvantage! Better yet, Scott knows how to fix it! Forever!

Finance industry? "It's the debt industry," as far as Scott is concerned, and he's been in trouble with money and credit in the past himself!

He learned all his secrets from the inside of the very industry he now rails against! Rather than perpetuating their abuse, he NOW works hard for neighborhood families and their financial turnarounds! He's been offered plenty of jobs at all the "big banks," and understandably so!

They want to put his knowledge to work for them, and keep him from

sharing it with their homeowner victims! But I won't take the bait," says Tucker.

This reporter recommends that you call Scott immediately so you won't ever have to be in this depressing hole of debt ever again!

You work hard, busting your hump to make your payments on time! You go to work every day, and you try not to

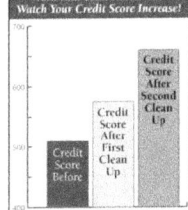

Work with Scott Tucker and Watch Your Credit Score Increase!

worry, but constantly the avalanche comes crashing down upon your head!

You're so busy trying to make your ridiculous minimum monthly payments, that you don't have any time at all available to spend learning the ins, outs, and secrets of the very system that holds you down!

Even if you keep up on the "debt industry" and fancy yourself a bit of an expert," there are a lot of things that you still don't know! That they would be horrified if you learned them! Scott chose years ago to help you overcome the barriers that were set in place purposefully, deliberately, and strategically to hold you down!

Scott will tell you about the home loan traps and crooked schemes financial corporations pull on unsuspecting people just like you every single day!

He can repair your credit for you, while you watch TV! He knows how to go about cleaning it up and boosting

your damaged credit score almost instantly!

Learn the truth about 'credit counseling'! Why is the Federal Trade Commission shutting those scamsters down? And dissolving their non-profit status?

Scott knows your creditors' methods of discriminating against you by using a computerized credit score!

He'll wipe out all your credit card balances, without filing for a bankruptcy! Or damaging your credit in any way!

He can get you better interest rates, and show you how to legally, morally, and ethically write off 100% of the interest you pay! Just like the "fat cats" do!

Even consumers with no credit at all can access more financial opportunities, thanks to Scott Tucker!

Could you handle getting 2 months no bills to pay? No mortgage? No car notes? No credit cards!

He'll build you a 100% legal, ethical, and moral "middle class tax shelter!" (Hint: This is the very same technique the wealthy already know about! And they've used it for decades!)

Why aren't you using it? You're throwing away thousands of dollars a year right there alone!

Want a new car? Hear Scott's secret information on why 0% car loans suck! And how to wipe-out your car loans! And get your titles back from the bankers free and clear! No more car payment! Now you can truly say, 'Its paid for!'

"I'll save you hundreds to thousands of dollars every month! Money you now throw down the toilet! Scott says. 'And not only that, but you'll live better than you do now! This is no 'coupon-clipping' type of thing!'

Is this guy for real? He claims he can get you as much as $200,000.00 in CASH! While still saving you money each month! 'I've even gotten folks more than that in the past,' he brags! 'Some only want $10,000 in cash! Or *(continued on Section A Page 2)*

(continued on Section A Page 2)

HOW TO PREVENT IDENTITY THEFT

By John Masui

The best way to prevent Identity Theft is always to be vigilant. Never assume or take things for granted. Here are examples of some of the steps you can take to protect yourself against Identity Theft.

• Buy a shredder–they are readily available from any office supplies company. They are also relatively cheap

compared to the cost of having your identity stolen.

• Do NOT throw bank statements, check books, utility bills or old credit cards in the trash. Always shred them or cut them up by using a pair of scissors.

• When paying for goods at a shop or withdrawing money from a cash point machine always protect your passwords, codes, PIN numbers from prying eyes.

• Protect your personal information within your own home. You may be careful about locking your doors and windows, and keep your personal papers in a secure place, but an identity thief may not need to set foot in your house to steal your personal information!

You may be storing your financial records, tax returns, birth date, and bank account numbers on *(continued page 8)*

(continued page 8)

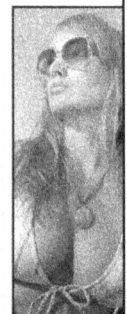
58

Chapter Four
You've Got It All Wrong

For decades now, people have mistakenly thought they need to cut price to gain sales; then they believe the they can "make it up in volume." But say you're selling a widget—a hard, physical product— not a service; and say your widget wholesale cost $50, and that you intend to sell this widget for $100. So, the most money you can make is $50. For now, we won't consider your other overhead.

Now say there's a guy who moves in next to you who is selling the same widget for $90. In that case, you decide to sell it for $80, and figure you'll "make it up in volume." Now, at $80, you can only make $30 per widget net profit, when you used to make $50. In reality, however, you'll have to sell almost *twice* as many widgets as you did at one hundred dollars to make the same amount of net profit!

This proves that it's not about volume; instead, it's about selling fewer widgets, but at higher retail prices. Instead of selling your $50 widget for $100, you are better off raising your prices to $110 but selling *fewer* widgets. In order to do this, you could also give folks other sort of intangible things that are hard for them to place a value on, and hard for your new neighbor to imitate. Such as a free class on proper widget use & safety, periodic widget owner cocktail parties, a barbeque each summer, who knows what. It might sound nuts to you, but if you pay attention, existing higher-end and "luxury" businesses currently do it all the time, all around you. Harley-Davidson does it. Disney does it. Apple does it. All 3 operate in categories with lots of cut-rate competitors, just as you do. But these 3 companies have totally de-commoditized their products and services! And as a result, Harleys, for instance, cost about *twice* what a comparable Japanese cruiser costs! And have you been to Disney lately?

The way you get this done in the mortgage business is to stop talking about the widget—the mortgage—and start talking about all the problems and emotions your prospective, current, and past borrowers have. What keeps them up at night? What worries and problems are driving them crazy? They have 'em, but you have to ask about them for them to let loose and tell you about it all. Then tell them how you can put all their fears and anxieties to rest, replacing them their problems with solutions and benefits. Keep the widget out of the conversation, and present *yourself* as the guru who provides a solution. Remember, they can't get *you* cheaper down the street! Everything else will take care of itself. The only thing you have to do is to keep your fees at the legal maximum, and your net income will take care of itself, and you won't be in any kind of "competition" with the guy next door, because the guy next door only sells "mortgages." Yuck.

Fee-cutting hurts your brokerage. Most mortgage brokers mistakenly think that they have no costs of goods and services, or that they have no cost to complete their mortgage refi's—just their time. Well, your time has to have the highest dollar value placed on it possible, and that is *impossible* with fee-cutting. If you discount from 5 points to 2 on a mortgage refi, you now have to do at least *two and a half times* the number of loans you used to have to do to make that 5 points of gross fee income! Do you wanna do more loans for less money? Really? You're better off to get rid of that 2-point price-shopping borrower and replace him with a properly cultivated non-rate and -fee sensitive 5-point borrower, so you can work less, and make more money! Desensitizing borrowers to fees is one of the most important things that needs to be done in your mortgage brokerage! And, it can be done with a proper mortgage marketing system that does not discuss rate and fee, but benefits, problem-solving, outcomes, and your guru status!

The Wal-Marts Never Last

Discounting is most prevalent in big box retail stores. But the memories of most folks are very short when it comes to this dead-end way of doing business, and the graveyard of dead discount retailers is very, very full. Let's not skip the homework of taking the time to read the tombstones. Many have gone down the tubes because they thought the way to make more money and stay in business was to cut price—Woolworth's, Sears, Montgomery Ward's, and K-Mart to name only 4 of the most recent in American history. One died-off completely. One withered badly. One sold their name to a mail-order only operator. And another is back from bankruptcy, but a pale comparison to Wal-Mart. Of course, the next to go down the tubes will be Wal-Mart. This cycle never ends, just the names change. Wal-Mart is at or very close to a peak. And we all know that you can only cut prices so far. At some point, you're at wholesale prices. And, don't forget labor, real estate, utilities, transportation, and all those other costs that most consumers never consider. Wal-Mart has a great supply chain thing going, but their answer to make more money is to keep wages down, which doesn't last forever. At some point, you can't pay less. You can only increase your bottom line by cutting expenses for so long. At some point, there's nothing left to cut. They've beaten up on their suppliers until they can give no more, and they're already pretty much at their breaking point. There are no further efficiencies to be gained by Wal-Mart, and as energy prices rise, their warehouse on wheels is becoming a bit of a problem for them. At some point, there will be a new "Wal-Mart" who will beat up on them and do things in an even more cost-effective manner than what they are doing now. It will be possible for the new "Wal-Mart," but the existing Wal-Mart will be unable to match it, just like K-Mart before them. And so it goes. Wal-Mart will go the way of all the other price cutters. The companies that *stay* in business are the ones that *raise* prices, and de-commoditize their widgets.

Let's take a closer look at K-Mart, which is a key example of discounting gone wrong. As a kid in the 70s, I went to K-Mart all the time. K-Mart has since gone bankrupt and has slowly gotten back into business. It's trying to find a place in a very crowded marketplace full of other discounters. The problem with K-Mart is that it really has no way to set itself apart from anyone. Maybe the store is closer to you, but if it's not, you're not going to drive past all the other discounters to get to a K-Mart. They foolishly even cut their Martha Stewart line, which gave them price insulation from others, and a celebrity endorsement. K-Mart tries to compete with Wal-Mart, but Wal-Mart is "always low prices." K-Mart's answer is, "Well, we're not quite as cheap as Wal-Mart, but we're pretty good most the time."

> When you discount your price and present yourself from the get-go as the low-cost provider, the level of respect and "compliance" you get from your borrower is immediately discounted as well.

You invite price-shopping and tire-kicking, and even hostile mistreatment from your borrowers. And you will very likely have higher per deal ad costs, because you'll have to do a higher volume of advertising to get a higher volume of leads, because the ones you get with "low price" offers and ads are far more fickle and fleeting than those drawn to you out of "guru status" from non-low price offers, ads, and marketing. Now, the ones you would get from *non*-low price offers are just a lot "stickier." That is, they "stick" around better. They aren't asking you "What are your rates?" and then hanging-up on you when you answer them. With low price offers and ads, you're doing "me-too" advertising and inviting prospective borrowers to shop you against the "competition," all the while, they will view you as a commodity that's interchangeable with any other "mortgage guy." Something they can get anywhere. With low price offers, you'll end up doing deals with no borrower loyalty, poor borrower relationship, at lower gross fees, and lower net profits per loan, if any at all. This will cause you to have to do far more deals, than the premium price provider does, to make your income goals. Price-cutting ads will cause overall advertising expenses to soar. Also, time spent with tire-kickers goes through the roof with low price offers. With low price offers, it will become challenging to stay in business even in a refi boom, no matter how fast you peddle. And during "tough times," you may as well just close up shop, if you insist upon the price-cutting route, because that makes net profits disappear in a hurry.

But when you charge top dollar, and present yourself as the problem-solving guru, an expert, and not a "mortgage guy," your perception in the eyes of your borrower is much, much higher. They no longer view you use a mortgage guy, and their compliance with your instructions is at the utmost.

How do you charge big fees? The best way is to "just do it." When you work up that refi transaction on your legal pad, which is the way I prefer, you put your appraised value, let's say $100,000, at the top. Then you put the maximum LTV the borrower qualifies for—let's say 85%. So $100,000 times .85 is $85,000 as the new loan amount. And you work in there for yourself a 5 or 7.99 points, building in your points before you build in anything else.

If the loan amount is $100,000 and you're in a 5-point capped state, your 5 points are of course $5,000. Now there's $95,000 left that goes toward the borrower's needs. If you're having any reluctance at all about charging big fees, then you should reevaluate your thinking that causes you to see charging a premium fee for a premium service as somehow "wrong." And, if you won't charge big fees, the borrower certainly isn't going to do it for you.

There is no "too much." The borrower, in our system, in America, has a responsibility of due diligence—*caveat emptor.* The borrower is to determine as a consumer what the right price is. If the borrower feels that the 5 points or 7.99 points is too much, they can go elsewhere—and I encourage you to let them, because you have to make "x" dollars per hour to meet your income goals. You can't waste time with cheap customers. There's no net profit in that. It's just silly busywork that does *not* result in net profit. Sure, you should do a good sales job on them, present them with all the problems you're solving, remind them subtly of all the emotions you're putting at ease with your problem-solving, and all the solutions you're providing that they didn't even know they needed. But beyond that, if they're just cheap, then they're just cheap and you're better off letting them go somewhere else. And oftentimes, they'll come back and apologize saying that you were right! They couldn't get what you said you offered anywhere else. And if they don't come back at all, that's just as well. Rely on your mortgage marketing system to create new borrowers for you who are *not* price-sensitive, who *will* pay you any legal fee you demand.

If you choose to compete in a me-too fashion, to cut price, and to present yourself to the marketplace as a mortgage guy rather than an expert financial problem-solver, you will get into the area of having to deal with shoppers who will ask you to cut your rate and fees, and that's a recipe for disaster. The brokers who play that game go out of business in a refi bust. And, you have a responsibility to your borrowers to be there to help them further in the future. You don't do anybody any service by going *out* of business.

Summary:

- You can't cut prices, and "make it up in volume." You'll just go broke.
- The less you charge, the less compliant and the more disrespectful your borrowers will be. And, referrals will suffer, too.

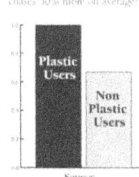

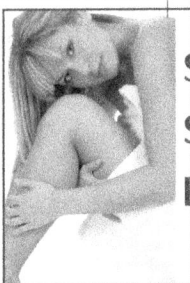

Chapter Five
Charge More

The stigma, I guess, that most consumers associate with mortgage brokers is someone who only wants them for that one transaction. It's sort of like a sleazy guy in a bar who only wants a one-night stand. And so most consumers either have the perception, or have heard the horror stories, of having done one transaction with a mortgage broker, and then never having heard from him again. "They don't call the next day."

That is exactly the *opposite* of what you should do. No matter how "relationship phobic" you may be in your romantic life, you should realize that long-term relationships are nothing but beneficial when it comes to your past borrowers! You have a huge opportunity before you because most others in the business do things the wrong way. You have the opportunity to utilize a Past Borrower Retention System® like the program I have created for my members, one that keeps in constant contact with them *automatically* and establishes a *real* friendship. Past borrowers stop viewing you as somebody they need to haggle with and start viewing you as a *friend* who's always there for them.

You can differentiate yourself by not doing marketing the same way everyone else does.

The me-too advertising that *most* mortgage brokers do is exactly what pigeon-holes them. They do it to themselves. They put themselves in a *price* competition with others, which causes them and their services to be viewed as a commodity folks can get anywhere; therefore borrowers have no reason to choose them above the others, and certainly no reason to pay the maximum legal fee for a refinance.

Differentiation is essential to make a high net income in the mortgage business. If borrowers can get exactly what you do somewhere else, why do you deserve to be in business, in existence, at all? No one needs left shoes. Is it because you've got a better handshake? A better business card? A nicer suit, or a fancier tie? Certainly, these aren't things that people want to pay more for. What they would like to pay more for is an *individualized* sort of "concierge" experience, an experience in which they feel that you know them inside and out. They feel that you understand all their problems, that you care, and that you're in-tune with their emotions. That you don't blame them for having made any past mistakes; that you don't point fingers; that you are only interested in moving things forward, and solving their problems for them.

Selling to the Simpsons

Basically, all people are Homer Simpson. You may laugh at that or think it's not true, but if you think about yourself, you have certain characteristics that are very much in line with Homer. So do all your friends, your parents, your siblings, and people you know in your community; this applies to very wealthy people and to very poor people—everybody's pretty much Homer Simpson. Everybody has their own little comfort zone and a few things that are important to them, and scores of things that are of no importance to them at all.

Most people don't do many new things in any given day. They just follow yesterday's patterns. They want their Duff beer when they get home; and they want things done for them, so that they don't have to think about them, or learn anything new. This creates a huge opportunity for a mortgage broker who has the 1-stop shop problem-solving attitude and marketing. When you use non-rate and fee mortgage marketing, the reason your borrowers don't realize that the tool you use to solve their problems is a mortgage, until they're already half-way done signing the disclosures, is because they really didn't want to *think* about it all in the first place. "Just fix this mess for me."

All borrowers, whether prime, non-prime, or reverse mortgage, share the same financial problems that 80% of Americans do. Prime are no "better" than non-prime. Reverses are no different than forwards.

Henry David Thoreau said, "**Most men lead lives of quiet desperation.**" This is true for just about everybody, white collar, blue collar, and senior alike. When we take into account the 80/20 rule, the lives of the 80-percenters are pretty ho-hum, boring, and routine. They do pretty much the same thing on Tuesday that they did on Monday. They work all year to get two weeks' vacation, or they work all year and then work overtime to try to keep up with their bills.

Everybody's pretty much dissatisfied with some part of life. So if, when you deal with borrowers, you treat them like royalty, as if they're the most important person in the world to you, and you "go the extra mile" (which is one of the principles from Napoleon Hill's book, *Think and Grow Rich*); if you do things for them that you're not expected to do and you give them those little extra touches that nobody else ever gives them; they will appreciate you a great deal. They will not view you as a mortgage guy because that's not what mortgage guys are known to do!

There's a place called Laskey's Auto where I grew up in Lansing, Michigan. When I was a kid, my mom took her car there to get worked on. Now this guy has a great big brand-new building with 10 or 12 bays. It's the biggest independent auto repair place you ever saw, and one of the reasons he's done so well is that he's famous for his customer service. Every day, he calls everybody individually who was in the shop the day before. Nowadays, it might be thirty or forty cars, but he still calls them up personally and says, "I wanted to give you a call, and see how your car's running today." More important than the feedback from customers is the fact that no other auto shop ever does that. Every time he calls somebody, and asks how their car is running, they tell ten people that, "The owner of Laskey's called me today to ask how my car is running!" Talk about some great free advertising! He never has to advertise, although he does a bit anyway, because he's got everybody else "advertising" for him! He has thousands of "salesmen" out on the streets working for him for free! All because he does that extra little touch each day.

At my urging, my members are famous for meeting with their borrowers at their offices for the application, and then, that very same day before going home, writing a handwritten thank-you card to the borrower and mailing it to them. Typically it's something like, "Thank you for trusting me to help your family with such-and-such." And, on the same day as the closing, my members order flowers to be sent to a woman's workplace, and/or steaks to be sent to a man's workplace. The reason why we send it to the workplace, is so everybody else *sees* it, and *asks* about it! Not only does the borrower feel appreciative to receive this free gift, but also all the people in the office are wondering why Susie got flowers today! "Geez, I wonder who sent those to her?" And then everybody else that Susie works with talks about my members! One good thing about the flowers and steaks is that they arrive during the rescission period, and if there is any feeling of buyer's remorse, or some thought that "maybe Scott was only after my money," those doubts are erased, and replaced with reassurance that you really do care, and that you meant everything you said.

If you charge more, that automatically means you are able to provide more, whether it's in time spent developing a sincere person-

> to-person relationship, having the extra
> money lying around to send them flowers
> and/or steaks, or an entertaining "theme-
> park" office environment.

You want your borrowers to see that you are more than just another loan guy. And then they really will feel that they are getting more than what they paid for.

They can have 2 out of the 3 of: best quality, lowest price, or best service; but they can't get all 3 at once. And so, I prefer to give them best quality, and best service, but they can't have lowest price, because that's simply not economically sustainable. No one should ever be surprised that when they go for the lowest price that they get the worst service. When they go for the highest price, however, they generally get the best service, which is what they really want. Beauty's in the eye of the beholder, and the only person who can determine whether the price is justified or not is the *borrower*. Not some grandstanding politician and not a "consumer advocate" who is never going to be your consumer.

So long as they feel they're getting more than they're giving, they're going to sign on the dotted line, and the transaction will take care of itself. Really, the brokers who have the hardest time making money in the mortgage business are the ones who discount the value of their own services! Remember that you're not your borrower, and you're not in *their* emotional state. You don't have their problems, and you're also not greedily looking at the solutions that they're going to get. But they are. You just have to have the testicular fortitude it takes to charge top dollar!

The worst mistakes mortgage brokers make are usually starting out with either no marketing, which is terrible, or even worse, using "me-too" marketing that positions them as a mortgage guy. Then, when they get the borrower to respond, they talk like a mortgage guy, using mortgage words that repel or even frighten the borrower. They get borrowers asking price questions, rate and fee, or they use all the same jargon that every other mortgage person uses. I encourage you to immediately change your vocabulary, come up with words that are *different* from those regularly used by others in the industry.

Other mistakes can be meeting with borrowers at home, rather than having the borrower come to you. First of all, when they come to your office, you have a home field advantage *psychologically*, in *their* eyes. A vacuum salesman goes door to door; mortgage brokers should not. This is also an image-management tool; you always want to be seen as the wise man atop the mountain. After all, people don't have their dentist come to their house! They go to their dentist's office! So position yourself like any other professional, knowledgeable, and respectable high-end financial service provider.

Summary:

- There is a mountain of money hiding in your past borrower list!
- You have to market yourself differently than everyone else in your marketplace.
- Treat your borrowers like royalty, because no one else ever does. Now, their dealings with you are the bright spots in their lives.
- When they feel they're getting more than they're giving, they'll pay you any legal fee you demand.
- Never meet a borrower outside of your own office.

Chapter Six
Rates Don't Matter and Neither Do Fees

Rates and fees are really irrelevant. Most of the time, borrowers have their finances set up in a very inefficient manner. Both from the standpoint of tax deductibility and in terms of a monthly cash flow. It's usually not very difficult to put a borrower in a better situation today than they were yesterday. Oftentimes, even if you're only doing a rate and fee refinance transaction, this is possible; but it's also of course possible with credit card debt and car loans. In a transaction that benefits the borrower's monthly cash flow, the rate and fee are only important if *you* make them seem so. If you advertise your mortgage refinance as a mortgage refinance, then you're going to get a lot of price buyer questions like "What's the rate, what are the fees?" Well, the rates and the fees do *not* matter; the *outcome* matters. If your borrowers are saving two hundred dollars a month, what do they care what the rate and fee are? I mean, are they shopping for problem solving and benefits or are they shopping for rate and fee? If they shop for rate and fee, they will probably end up with the worst mortgage broker, who is just scraping by, and probably quite incompetent. That's why those questions have no place in the process.

> You make rates and fees irrelevant by marketing your mortgage refinance as something *other* than a mortgage refinance, such as marketing *yourself* as a problem solver.

When *you* are the thing that solves their problems, they have to come to *you,* and can go *nowhere* else! You play to the borrower's problems, their fears, their anxieties, and present yourself as the problem-solver that makes all that go away. You present them with all sorts of benefits that they desire, and even benefits that they didn't yet know they needed! I mean, that's how the iPhone was marketed, right? You didn't even know you needed it until Apple told you so! Make the borrower feel totally taken care of. The idea of you making money off them leaves their minds, and they trust you to handle the whole transaction, as *you* see fit, just as soon as they feel that you care for them, and that you're handling all their needs for them, without any heavy lifting on their part. All questioning, interference, and haggling has been removed from the process. It's so much easier when the sale isn't an argument, but rather something that happens seemingly automatically.

You know, a lot of people in the mortgage business like to talk about how much loan *volume* they do. Well, if you don't get to take home loan *volume* at the end of the day as your compensation, then why even talk about it? When LOs talk about how they did twenty-seven loans this month, all I have to say is that doing 27 loans in a month would make me want to shoot myself! I'd rather do five a month and get 5 to 7.99 points on each transaction, than to do 27 loans for a half point a piece!

With direct response marketing, there are ways to make sure you *only* get *above average* loan amounts. I prefer a high-end Homer Simpson, a sort of high blue-collar, low white-collar kind of borrower, that's a *commonsense* person not a nitpicker, who just wants their problems solved. If you're getting 5 points or 7.99 points per transaction, doing 5 of those deals per month, working 20 hours a week with everything *automated* and *systemized* with maybe one part-time assistant, then you're off to the races!

Snowflakes Are Different; Businesses Are Not

Everybody has the idea that their business is different, that what other businesses employ in direct marketing can't work for their business. Maybe this is true if you're selling pencils door-to-door, or something like that, but when you're in the mortgage business, you're in one of the highest transaction businesses there is. Other similar industries are life and health insurance, or perhaps yacht or luxury car sales, but mortgages and real estate are pretty much the highest value transactions most people are ever going to deal with. And the higher the transaction value, the more *useful* emotional direct response marketing can be. You're only limited by your *imagination,* which Albert Einstein said was "more important than knowledge"—and he was right!

An emotional direct marketing system reaches the homeowner *directly*, skipping over any "meddlers," such as realtors and attorneys that might normally get in your way without such a direct marketing system. You avoid ever having to do a deal with realtors involved at all, by going straight to the existing homeowner. Then you present the homeowner with the problems you already know they have, and you present *yourself* as their problem-solver, a specialist at resolving these issues for them. When you're perceived as the expert that can solve all their problems, you're in the driver's seat! And you're now able to out-earn every *other* mortgage broker in your area! Direct response marketing is *not* something you have to do for yourself, but if you're not going to do it yourself, you have to have somebody very knowledgeable about the task at hand, preferably someone with experience in the mortgage brokerage business just like you. I am just such a person, and I provide a mortgage marketing system that you can find out about at **www.MortgageMarketingGenius.com**.

The most common challenge I hear from mortgage brokers is that they "can't get enough business"—or if they can get enough business, that "everybody's a price shopper." If they can't get enough business, it's either because they have no mortgage marketing system at all, or one that presents them as a commoditized "me-too" mortgage guy. If they have enough business, but not enough *well-paying* business, with high gross fees, and high net profits per deal, then the problem is that they're advertising based upon rate and fee, or just as a "mortgage refinance provider," or their dealing with realtors on purchases, and in any event, pigeon-holing themselves.

My system can work for anyone. What's important is an understanding of emotional direct response marketing, of business, and of pricing for net profitability… and also some understanding of salesmanship. The Tucker Mortgage Marketing System® can work for *anyone,* it's just a matter of working smarter, not harder.

Direct response marketing, in a very non-pushy way, talks to people in the frame of mind in which they already find themselves. "The Robert Collier Principle" is that you need to enter the conversation that's already occurring inside the prospect's mind. Effective direct response marketing for your mortgage business is no different. It needs to "catch" the borrower in the conversation they're *already* having in their own mind. It then needs to continue that conversation with the prospective borrower; the very same conversation they've been having with themselves for the past few days. The talk they have with themselves about all of their problems, their emotions; and, in a very empathetic way, your mortgage marketing needs to never accuse them of having done anything wrong, even if they have. Then, your mortgage marketing need to point to you as the "fix it man," without ever painting you as a mortgage guy.

Once you stop price-cutting your services, and stop presenting yourself as an interchangeable widget that borrowers can get anywhere, you're finally able to charge maximum fee, and make maximum money in minimum time.

You're able to get your life back, your family life back, prevent divorce, keep custody of the kids, and not have your assets split in half. You actually make *more* than you've ever made and work *less* than ever. And you get to help people in exactly the manner they want to be helped, pleasing your borrowers more than you ever have. But this is only possible if you'll step outside of "the mortgage business" and view *yourself* as a *marketer* of services that solve people's problems, not as a mortgage guy who chases after deals in an act of desperation.

Summary:

- Loan volume is useless.
- Use your direct response marketing to cut out realtors and attorneys.
- If you advertise "rate and fee" all you'll get is price-shoppers.

ADVERTISEMENT

ion A — CONSUMER FINANCE — December 2007

SUMER
Y I N G
DLINES

ons
made a purchase didn't
eed. It could have been
on and their pushy
rice was simply to good
many times have we
l said. "I wish I hadn't

re some guidelines to
opping to ensure you
the regret of making
purchase
rrive at the store know
u want and how much
o pay
knowledgeable about
u are thinking about
uld ask someone you
y member or friend
osts, the temptation to
on impulse or under
ch the product you
o online and search the

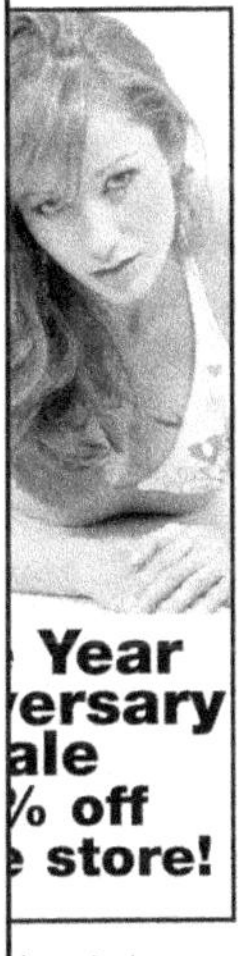

d price. Read consumer
ie product. Find a
e you expect to pay.
the company you are
unfamiliar with the
local consumer affairs
usiness Bureau
he company's return
fix items in house? Do

"Federal government acts to freeze interest rate hikes!"

Chicago -- The housing-induced "credit crunch," falling dollar, increasing food prices, sky-high oil-prices, has all been squeezing America's hard-pressed home owners!

In this mess, there is no one hit harder than our nation's home owners, who are now, house-by-house, suffering the pain of a mortgage interest rate reset. Added to that, it's now known that credit card companies are hiking interest rates and payments amounts even to those who have been paying on time.

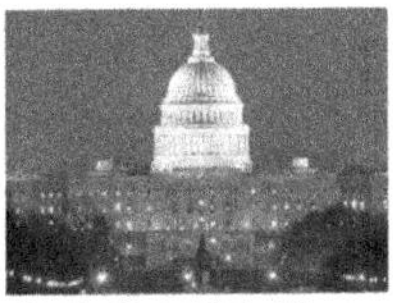

President Bush & Federal Reserve Chairman Bernanke, "finally, the federal government is acting to freeze mortgage interest rates!"

This "freeze" is just in time, saving home owners from this mess before it can get any worse.

Federal Reserve Chairman, Ben Bernanke, estimates that 450,000 home owners are set to experience a mortgage interest rate hike every 3 months! Without this "freeze," that's millions of Americans annually that were about to be stuck with increasing interest rates, with no way to avoid the hikes.

American families are already cash-strapped by rising food and energy prices, a falling dollar, increasing costs of important goods, you name it.

Now, thousands of American home owners are now being caught by shock and surprise, as their mortgage interest rates "re-set!"

Even formerly "on-time" home owners are finding they're unable to make ends meet in this environment of increasing interest rates & payments on their mortgages and credit cards. Added to that, states, counties, and municipalities are hiking property tax rates in real dollars, even as property *values* stagnate!

With these would-be mortgage and credit card interest rate hikes running rampant *nationally*, this is of course, no longer a "local" problem. National mortgage lenders are making up for "soft spots" in the U.S. housing market by hiking rates nationally. For every American they can.

Just as when a Hurricane Katrina hit New Orleans, and folks all across the country got hit with home owners' insurance rate hikes! The "fat cat" mortgage lenders are making up *their* short-falls by sending the bill for *their* mess to those who had nothing to do with it!

Some areas where home appreciation seemed it would never end, such as Florida and California, for example, some of the biggest spikes in foreclosures are occurring. And this only *adds* to the problem of mortgage lenders "passing the check" to those who did *nothing* wrong in the first place: you, the hard-working American home owner!

And in some areas foreclosures are running at a rate of one foreclosure for every 31 households! Thank goodness the feds are finally stepping in to help.

The media portray people who've suddenly found themselves in financial trouble, with increasing interest rates and higher monthly payments, as having "bad credit," with being "poor risks," and being otherwise "unwise" with their money.

But that stereotype is just not true. Millions of smart, hard-working, financially-savvy Americans have found themselves in a sudden set of circumstances that are not their faults! Anyone could have been affected by all this, and that's why so many have.

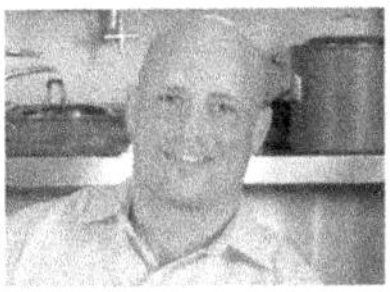

Chicago's Scott Tucker, "I make it so the big banks can't hike your mortgage & credit card interest rates!"

Thankfully, for the millions caught in this quagmire, there is hope, says Chicago's outspoken & unconventional consumer advocate, financial expert, and "Miracle worker," Scott Tucker.

Tucker says, "the 'credit crunch,' and housing market problems, mean it's hard for hard-working, cash-strapped American home owners to make their payments. Or even to sell their homes."

He says, "folks feel 'trapped' in a home they can't sell, and they're being squeezed for higher monthly [mortgage and credit card] payments! It's unfair, abusive, and it's not their faults!"

Tucker says, "in California alone October 2007 foreclosures increased by 40% from September! The big banks have foreclosed on a total of 12,336 properties, accounting for a loan value of $5 billion dollars! That's a 568% increase over the same period in 2006!"

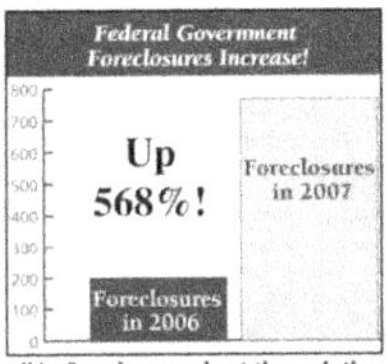

"As foreclosures shoot through the roof, the federal government, and Chicago's own Scott Tucker, are trying to get the message out to folks that these foreclosures need not happen at all! "There is an easy solution to this problem!" says Tucker."

Tucker is *furious* that, "predatory mortgage and credit card lenders have taken advantage of honest, hard-working Americans." Tucker says, "ordinary families are being abused by these big banks and lenders."

Tucker continues, "if you're in this tough spot now, you need to know that you do not have to put-up with their rising mortgage and credit card interest rates and payments any longer!"

"It's important to understand that the secrets I use on your behalf work for you whether you have good credit or bad!" he says. "If you've been hit by one of their unfair and abusive interest rate increases, I can fix it for you! No matter how bad it seems right now, there is a way out!"

He continues, "best of all, my solution for you does not involve 'credit counseling,' bankruptcy, and you don't have to sell your house! Just imagine all your debt and credit card problems

PERSONAL FINANCE - HAVE CONSUMERS HAD A BELLY FULL OF PERSONAL DEBT?

By Rachel Lane

For months, we were trigger-swipe happy, putting our groceries, clothes, holidays and service charges on our credit cards. We wanted mortgages, we took out loans, we watched Property Ladder and What Not To Wear. Whether you were born middle class, had middle class aspirations, you became middle class through your spending. Debt united people around the UK, we sympathised with each

Section A, Page 2   **CONSUMER FINANCE**   Decembe

Federal government acts to freeze interest...

fixed, darn-near overnight! No more car notes, no more credit card payments...you even get a 2 months with no bills to pay!"

Tucker says, "That alone will keep up to $15,270.48 in pre-tax income in your pocket! Not handed-over to the banks and 'fat cat' lenders! I even build for you your own 100% legal, ethical, & moral 'middle class tax shelter,' using tax 'loopholes' the rich have been using successfully for decades! And the IRS doesn't have a thing to say about it. It's 100% legal, using their own Internal Revenue Code!"

"By doing this for you, I save you _thousands_ of dollars in _unnecessary_ taxes! It's all done for you. And no, you do not need 'credit counseling,' do not have to go bankrupt, and you _get to keep your house_! I can even put some much-needed cash in your pocket left-over! Again, 100% tax free! It's all 100% legal, as I said! In fact, I do it every day!" says Tucker.

"Most folks who find their mortgage and credit card interest rates going up, think their situation is 'hopeless!' And a lot of the time that's because they've been 'turned-down' and denied help from their mortgage company, and the credit card companies, right when they need it _most_. They made all their payments for so long, but the mortgage companies and credit card companies have absolutely no sense of gratitude! Not even a sense of doing what's right by folks in need," Tucker fumes.

"But it doesn't matter what you've been told or led to believe, or how 'bad' you think your situation is right now. Because my simple solution wipes-out your money problems darn-near overnight!" says Tucker.

"It's not 'hard' at all. Well, it's hard

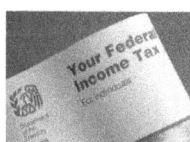

Tucker says, "You're over-paying on your income taxes, and your CPA or tax preparer doesn't even know it themselves! I use the tax code to build you a 100% legal, ethical, & moral 'middle class tax shelter!' And the IRS won't give you a moment's hassle about it, because I follow their code!" says Tucker.

for me, but easy for you. In fact, it's all done for you, and you're out of the mess you've recently found yourself in darn-near overnight!" he says.

And it's true. More and more home owners, who have found themselves stuck with increasing interest rates on their mortgages and credit cards are hitting-back at their greedy "predatory lenders," and refusing to be victims of their system any longer.

"Folks are realizing it's just not fair treatment, and that they don't have to take it. Not for another minute. They're relieved to learn of my system, and to find that it's 100% legal, ethical, & moral," says Tucker.

Tucker is adamant, "but if you choose to 'stuck your head in the sand,' instead of taking advantage of this 'gift horse' things can not get any better for you. You have to take the _first_ step. After that, it's as simple as the 'easy Button!' No, ignoring it, or pretending it isn't happening won't make it go away. _Procrastination_ will only make it worse, but action will fix it!"

"There is a way out, but you've got to take advantage of it before it's no longer possible. Congress could change the tax code at any time, for example. My system for preventing your interest rate increases could be gone _tomorrow_. We just don't know. The only thing we do know is that now is the perfect time to act!" he says.

Tucker continues, "You can bet those 12,136 families in California, whose homes were foreclosed upon in October, were 'hoping,' 'wishing,' and 'praying' things would just _somehow_ turn-out right, if they just kept-on pretending that it wasn't happening."

"It's a real shame for those folks, and a clear warning for others who are facing mortgage and credit card interest rate increases. No doubt about it, these rate increases are a knock-out blow to so many American home owners. But _only_ if they let it happen, and refuse my help," says Tucker.

He puts it this way: "If you've just had the shock of an interest rate increase, or if you're finding there's no longer enough money to pay your monthly bills...and if you're lying awake at night worrying about how you're going to make this month's bills, then you need to get it _fixed_, and you need to get it _fixed_ now, before it's too late!"

"It's insane, in my opinion, to not take my help and just keep on struggling through it all 'the hard way.' Paying more & more to those thieves each and every month. The saddest call

"I can help you now, but please don't wait until I can't help any longer!" says Tucker

I ever get, is from someone who turned-me down on my offer to help, but now finds the sheriff at their door, with the locksmith and moving crew in tow. That breaks my heart, but on that day, it's finally too late for me to be able to help," he says.

"Please don't let them get your house. For that matter, don't let them get your car. Don't let them cut off your credit cards. Don't let the bankruptcy sharks get a hold of you. I can prevent it all, but you have to accept my help," Tucker says.

Tucker concludes, "every month that goes by with you _still_ paying their rip-off interest payments, is just another month of fear, uncertainty, & doubt that need not be. It's no way to live. Especially when you could so much more easily get this all taken care of. Without nosey 'credit counseling,' embarrassing bankruptcy, and without having to try to sell your house! You do _not_ have to lose one thing that you've worked so hard for! Unless, that is, you refuse my help!"

To escape the burden of your rising interest rates, call Scott Tucker's 24 hour-a-day, 7 days-a-week, "eavesdrop hotline!" There won't be a live person to "bother" you. You'll just listen to his 100% FREE recorded message! The number to call to "eavesdrop" on Scott is 1-800-xxx-xxxx, press 1, then extension 9000!

If you prefer to research Mr. Tucker online, you may do so at www.MemberWebsite.com There, he has even more information on his system, complete with case studies of _other_ folks _just like you_ that he has helped, and **you may even apply online for his help!**

To reach Scott Tucker at his office, you may call 773-xxx-xxxx, or toll-free at 1-800-xxx-xxxx. (Some use the toll-free number to call from work, from a pay phone, or even from the neighbor's house after the phone's been shut-off.)

AMERICAN ARE SHOR DISCIPLIN COMES TO WITH THE

By Ed Bagley Like a 4- child at the check American consumers w to make their buying d more expensive it is, th

Here is an examp businessman shells o vehicle which costs ab He and his wife are to effort to have fun while

His comment on th dress rehearsal for nothing." Those big tea might well come fro inheritance fading awa mom.

Like a dog in heat, in America.

All of this impulse b Today article with this h the 4th of July". And i

Although the media

Life cha your sk Restore

CardTrack.com.

"Never have Americ toys, been faced with are so hard to control, psychology and autho Broke. Why Americans

The fact is that w anything we want anyt we want. Sellers and about selling us what cannot afford and a eventually drive us inte

Sellers and lenders have raised this willing expense to an air form

BUDGETING CAN MINIMIZE YOUR NEED TO BORROW

By: Ivan mantelli

Budgeting is an important aspect of finance and the better your budget is the lesser the requirement for loans A

well managed budget can become your all important tool especially when it comes to debt management. If your budget is sound then it will help you to

keep a track of your daily or monthly expenditures and you will also be able to keep a tab on your loans if any

There are many people who suffer as

84

Chapter Seven
Operations

Most of us who start out in the mortgage business begin as loan officers, oftentimes with little or no processing support. We usually have very limited sales training, marketing support, or even loan origination instruction from someone more experienced, let alone someone truly successful and accomplished. More often than not, we're just given a desk and a desk phone and told to *somehow* make some money.

You can see, then, how we might get in the mindset that we have to do *everything* ourselves. However, when you're able to move beyond that way of thinking, when you start to employ a mortgage marketing system like the one I've discussed, you'll find that instead of having more hours in each day than you have serious and committed borrowers, that you'll have more borrowers each day than there are hours in the day! And it's at that point that you'll want to have an assistant to help take some of the grunt work off your back. Ideally, once you teach them, bit by bit, week by week, and month by month, you should be able to delegate very easily all of your grunt work. After about a year, you'll find that you've created "a second you," in that that person can work their 40 hours, and those are 40 hours that you don't have to work! Now, you can do only the work that only you can do, which is pretty much only the marketing and sales, and you won't have to even come anywhere close to 40 hours a week, unless you really want to. It's not unusual, with an assistant, and by using the automated systems I teach, to find yourself working only 20 hour weeks, or far less!

Automation, of course, can be very beneficial to the mortgage brokerage business, just as it has been to other businesses. Since the first wheel and pulley or set of gears, there have been countless automations through all different forms of manufacturing and processing. Before McCormick invented the horse-drawn mechanical reaper, farmers used to have *half* the productivity they did with it. His company then became International Harvester. You may have heard of them.

So why not apply automation to a service industry, such as the mortgage industry? You can quite easily have a dedicated call center use your inbound lead taking script, so that when your prospective borrowers call in, having been cultivated by your automated mortgage marketing system, they think they're calling *your* office, when in actuality, they're calling a call center, and your "assistant" goes through the entire 20-question lead-taking script for you! These "mini-apps" are then e-mailed to you! These 20 questions get you started, providing you with a great deal of information on the borrowers. You can have the deal all worked-up by the time you first talk to them! My members use my copyright-protected 20-question lead-taking script to collect Social Security numbers and dates of birth as well! The script that comes with my Tucker Mortgage Marketing System® is a great resource, as I have tweaked it to obtain all the information you need.

Another form of automation is a website that folks are driven to, by your offline marketing. There they can see additional video testimonials from people that you've helped in the past, and more information about you and the ways you're able to help them. Then they're invited to apply online. Of course, just as with a call center, they can apply online 24 hours a day, 7 days a week.

Free recorded messages are another great
form of automation you can employ.

A great one would be a past borrower interview/testimonial. It might last maybe 15 minutes or so. At the beginning of the recording, the borrower is informed that if at any time they want to talk to you live they can just press zero. However, when you have them zero out, it's best to forward that call to your call center as well! So you're never actually taking *any* inbound lead calls yourself! Now, isn't that a better way to use your time?

If you employ the system that I've just detailed for you, you'll have *all* of your inbound lead calls taken by the call center 24/7 and your website operates around the clock as well, also e-mailing you're their applications! Life's too short to be sitting at a desk all day, or interrupted every minute on your cell phone, taking calls that could quite easily be taken by someone else, or gathering information that could automatically be collected by your website! Who wants to work more they have to? Not me! For more information on the Tucker Mortgage Marketing System®, you'll want to visit www.MortgageMarketingGenius.com, and request my free audio CD, free e-book, free faxed report, and a free telephone call with me.

More Timesaving Options

There are only so many hours in a day and you don't get any more hours than anyone else. The way to get a leg-up is time management. The call center, the website testimonials and loan application, and the free recorded message, are all ways to fully-automate your inbound lead-taking process, to where you're freeing up tons of your time, and no one in your office has to do any of this work. You don't need an employee to operate *any* of these systems.

Another way to free up your time is to have an in-office or out-of-office processor. If in-office, you might only need this person part-time. If out-of-office, someone on a contract, per file basis may be best. If in-office, this person certainly doesn't need much mortgage industry experience starting out; in fact, I'd encourage you to hire someone who has very little, if any, as they're less likely to have accumulated bad habits from other brokerages and past "inside the box" mortgage industry experiences. Besides, they can learn what they need to from a couple continuing ed. classes. You want somebody who has some initiative to figure things out on their own when possible, and someone who has a bit of drive to them. If you choose someone new to the business, the continuing ed. courses at your state brokerage association will give them the basics they need, and then you can teach them to abide by *your way* of doing business instead of using the same old tired jargon and gimmicks that other brokers use. The very words that turn borrowers off, and make them view you as a commodity. This processor needs to know how to say things in a way that borrowers are pleased to hear them. If you don't know what I mean here, then I encourage you to study Tom Hopkins' sales methods. All this is why I encourage you to find someone who's new to the mortgage industry. You want this person to facilitate the buying process, not make it more difficult. Someone who works with you to make the process a "greased slide" that the borrower slides down *effortlessly*, while making you large commissions in the process.

An enormous part of this business is trust. You have to trust the people you hire, you have to trust the processes of my Tucker Mortgage Marketing System® as I've described them, and your borrowers have to trust you.

As for process, when hiring is done with some forethought, you're able to entrust others to handle the grunt work.

If you own your own brokerage, some grunt work you should delegate is check writing, but not check-signing. However, this should be delegated to a CPA firm or bookkeeper. They should do all the tedious accounting work for you, but you should still have your bank statements delivered to your home, and you should still review them yourself, to make sure there's no funny business. I trust my CPA and her bookkeeping staff to do several tasks for me, with me spot-checking things along the way, just to make sure we keep everyone honest. Meet with your bookkeeper twice a month to sign the checks yourself. Or, have them FedEx'd to you for you to sign. You can then check your bank statements to make sure that all the checks that cleared were checks that you signed. You can also see if there have been any irregular debits from your accounts.

Something else you should delegate is the legal stuff, and by that I mean that you shouldn't just have an employee deal with yours for you. Above all else, make sure to pay attention to your marketing, your bookkeeping, and your legal stuff. You don't want to get too far from any of those, but you can certainly delegate the day-to-day grunt work of your mortgage business to processor/assistant as you would in any office. Just make sure that when they're processing the loan documents that they understand the way *you* do business is *different* from everyone else, and that they *never* discuss terms with borrowers. Their answer to those "terms" questions should be, "I don't know, but I can have Scott call you back with an answer." This way, your processor never blows a deal for you.

As I've already described, having an inbound lead-taking process, that streamlines and automates everything for you, frees up an enormous amount of your time. With a mortgage marketing system that drives you a lot of leads, if you don't have the automated inbound lead systems I've described, to take all the leads for you, you're going to have probably 20 or so hours a week just talking to these inbound prospective borrowers calling your office from your mailings, freestanding inserts ("FSIs"), niche publication display ads, door hangers, etc. And that, of course, is a lot of time spent, unnecessarily and ineffectively, on the phone with leads that could and should be handled in a smarter, automated fashion. Automating things so that inbound leads go to your dedicated call center with the 20-question inbound lead-taking script, having a 24-hour free recorded message with the zero-out function from the free recorded message to the call center, having a website that's able to take leads online from folks who respond from offline marketing, having this 24/7 ability, *and* having it all done by somebody else—not by you—is *essential* in managing your time. That's a big part of how my members are able to have 20 hours a week more free time than even somebody who has a government job.

My member brokers employ my system by simply plugging their name and contact information into the components and marketing pieces. The automatic lead-taking system I provide for my member brokers has been enormously beneficial to each of them. One member, in Maryland, who employed my systems, listened very carefully to me regarding delegation and systemized that as well. As a result, he was able to reduce his working hours to just 5 hours per week, and still make $80,000.00 a month. This gentleman was a realtor and not a loan officer before he joined my program. What was good about that is that he didn't know *anything* about mortgage business. So, he didn't go off in his own direction, follow old, failed patterns, and he didn't "over-think" things either. He simply chose to do everything *my* way. Just paint-by-number. And I think you and I can agree that 5 hours a week is *less* than *most* people work in a day! Yet 5 hours became the length of his working hours per week! And his monthly income of $80,000.00 per month is more than most people make in a *year!* Those results speak for themselves.

Growing Your Business

Starting any business *without* a plan is lunacy, especially in the mortgage business. Because you have to have some idea of how're you going to finance it *after* startup. Now, it doesn't need to be really complicated. I first financed my brokerage with an $11,000 balance on a Discover card. This was to pay for the first $5,000 mailing, and $6,000 worth of emotional direct response marketing mail-order courses, home office furniture, and home office equipment. I was able to generate $75,000.00 in fee income, which paid off everything, and left me with enough capital to send out another $5,000 mailing. Not only did my new business run out of the kitchen of my then 1-bedroom condo, but also in the first month I became debt-free, and turned a healthy profit. The point is, I had a *plan* for how I was going to finance my business, not only getting started, but the return-on-investment from that first mailing, that would finance my business *after* startup.

The second point is that I had a plan for how my mortgage marketing system was going to work. I knew that an offline sales letter mailed directly to folks who needed my help could then send them online to a website with additional testimonials, and an online application. Although, I'd only mention the additional online testimonials in the mailing, then the online application would happen, "by accident," in the borrower's mind. But the point is, it'd happen, and I'd get their info without having to take a live call.

Elements that have to be in your plan in order to grow are, of course, all the systems that I've discussed already: the call center, the 24-hour free recorded message, and the website for online applications. But to actually *grow*, you need to have the commercial office space where you can have an assistant/processor handle your files. This is a place where you can meet with your borrowers, so it's on your turf, not theirs. As I mentioned earlier, this gives you the home field advantage, but it also puts you in the driver's seat because it promotes your image of not only being a guru, but a successful guru. Nobody wants to do business with a bargain basement "me-too" mortgage guy; they want to deal with a professional, and I've got news for you: professionals have their own office and they have staff, and because of this, they get respect.

The first step you should take to make growth happen in your mortgage brokerage is to get a mortgage marketing system if you don't currently have one. You need a program that is going to funnel borrowers directly to you for a mortgage refinance. You can no longer depend on realtors, and you never should have become dependent upon them in the first place. It's always bad to "need" anything. Always remember that. "Realtor-dependence" is a habit that needs to be broken. That means no more purchase loans, only refi's.

The next step you take is to *automate* every aspect of the inbound lead-taking process.

This involves writing your inbound 20-question lead-taking script, including a way to get Social Security numbers and dates of birth. Additionally, set up 24-hour free recorded message hotlines, with past borrower testimonial interviews, that you've conducted yourself, over the telephone, with a cheap, $100 phone recorder. You have past borrowers, and someone in that filing cabinet of yours has to be happy with what you did for them, so get to it! In the recording, encourage folks to press zero at any time during the interview to talk to you live. When they press zero, they'll actually be forwarded to your call center, so that they can take the lead for you, and then it will be e-mailed to you and your assistant. Isn't this a better way to do business? No more 40 hours a week spent working the phones. No more long evenings at the office. Once your assistant receives the e-mailed lead, which is yours and yours alone, they're able to work it up. They can do all the drudgery of checking the person's credit, checking the home value, prequalifying with the lender, all those things…and even working up the deal for you, before you even call the borrower back! Then when you do call them, which your website, or your call center already told them was going to take you at least 24 business hours, you'll find that not only have they been patient, but that they're just glad to talk to you. When's the last time a borrower was giddy to talk to you? What's funny about this is that they're going to say "yes" to any sensible solution to their problems that you pitch them. This is because they've been trying to get to you, not your assistant, for at least a day or so. Thanks to having this system in place, the first time you talk to them, you have a deal all worked-up for them. You can have your assistant call to turn down the "turn-downs."

When you call them back, what you say will sound something like this: "Homer and Marge, I know you have these 3 heavy concerns that you told my assistant about the other day, and yes, I found those to be evident in my research, but I also found these 7 additional problems, that you may or may not even be aware of…" You go through how you can help resolve all of these problems, and then say, "And here are the 18 benefits that my fast action plan will provide to you. I know you weren't even asking for these things, maybe because you thought them to be impossible for you, but I think that after I've described them to you, that you'll share my enthusiasm for what I'm able to do for your family." Of course, these benefits are just thrown in as icing on the cake. When you present them with this fast action plan, and their response will be, "Great! So what do we do next?!"

You schedule them for an appointment, to come into your office, and sign off on some "paperwork." The whole reason to have them come to your office is because they have to move *towards* you. And once they've moved towards you, and followed your command, they won't stop being compliant with your commands. Isn't this better than you going to their house, and giving the impression that you're in the business of chasing deals out of desperation? If you go to their house, you're just asking for a kick in the teeth. When you meet with them at the office, you are in complete control and they'll easily sign the disclosures without a second thought. Sure, you could have FedExed the doc's to them, but this should never, ever be considered. That's a big reason why the me- too guys have trouble with their fees! Because they short-cut things, take the easy way out, and they don't get a face-to-face meeting on their own turf, where they can point out all the pain and problems the borrower has, and then explain all the benefits that they're able to bestow to the borrower. Once you've done things exactly this way, you'll find that getting 5 to 7.99 points on *every* mortgage refinance is no challenge at all.

Summary:

- You need to delegate to get more done in less time.

- You can use free recorded messages, and websites, to have your best past borrowers sing your praises for you!

- You can use a call center to run your inbound lead-taking script, and get you applications with SSNs & DOBs without you ever talking to another inbound lead!

Section A	CONSUMER FINANCE	January 2008

HOW TO CHOOSE THE BEST GAS CARD

Tim Tessin

Everyone in today's world loves to ... The only downfall when it comes to ... ng is the expenses it comes with from ... renance to gas. What if there was a ... o save money at the pump every time ... lled up? If it sounds too good to be ... it isn't.

today's society, especially with the ... net, its very seldom that you need to ... ull price for anything anymore. The ... goes for gas. Credit card companies ... a range of reward based credit cards ... nclude savings on gasoline. The nice ... about these gas credit cards are that ... able to save so much per gallon.

you're unfamiliar how gas credit cards ... its not a hard process to understand ... A gas credit card is simply a credit ... with a reward. It's no different than a ... that gives cash back or bonus airline

Join Now!

embership all Now for details!

It simply gives back a percentage of ... fill-up. Almost every gas credit card ... take off a certain percentage per ... t. For instance, the BP Visa credit ... will take off ten percent per gallon for ... rst ninety days. If the current price is ... dollars a gallon, you're only going to ... to pay $2.70. That's a savings of thirty ... per gallon? You can only imagine

"If you already have an 'FHA' mortgage, now this safe, federal government program slashes your mortgage payment! Quick & easy!"

Chicago—In recent months, things have gotten tough for millions of hard-pressed American homeowners. A worldwide "credit crunch," a falling American Dollar, and record oil-prices...all have conspired against us.

Stuck in the middle of this mess are millions of hard-working American home owners. And no one has been hit harder by this sudden economic turn-of-events than the "FHA" mortgage holder.

Because as well as being squeezed by higher prices for almost everything in the stores...food, gas...you name it...many are now struggling to meet their monthly FHA mortgage payments.

Even home owners who've always managed to pay on time are now finding it harder and harder to make ends meet. "Too much month left at the end of the money," as the saying goes.

For many families, it seems only a matter of time before something has to "give" and they start getting seriously behind on their payments; something that's happening with increasing frequency all over the U.S. And late payment so often leads to one thing...foreclosure.

The talking heads on TV portray good, hard-working people just like us who've suddenly found ourselves struggling to meet our FHA mortgage payments as "irresponsible." Well, we're anything but! It's because of unfairly high interest rates, and increasing costs for everything we have to buy just to live, that we've found ourselves in tough times.

But these negative stereotypes are really put out by the real culprits in all this: the big, fat, greedy corporate titans, "predatory lenders," and other crooks who really pay the salaries of the talking heads, either by network ownership, or by their advertising dollars and their money's influence.

And don't forget who finances the campaigns of the politicians as well. They're told what to say just the same as the newscasters.

No, it's those who've mismanaged

FORECLOSURE NOTICE

KEEP OUT

"The biggest mistake you can make is wait until you NEED help to ask for help!"

the stock market, hedge funds, and all that that have brought about all our problems in the economy today. And now they're trying to pass-on the costs of clearing-up their messes to us FHA mortgage borrowers.

Just the same as when Enron went bust thanks to the greed, mismanagement, outright thievery of the executive "fat-cats" siphoning off the money! When it all falls apart, as it always does, they turn to Uncle Sam to bail them out with our income tax dollars! We're footing the bill, and left to clean-up their messes!

"Scott Tucker uses this 'Secret' safe, federal government program to save you lots of cash!"

Truth is, any FHA home owner struggling to make their FHA mortgage payments in the face of the sudden economic storm is really blameless in all this, because millions of smart, hard-working, financially-savvy FHA home owners Americans have found themselves suddenly dropped into messy financial circumstances through no fault of our own!

"Anyone could have been affected by all this, and that's why so many have!"

But it's not all bad news, at least not for FHA home owners! That's thanks to a newly-uncovered "secret" federal government program that is slashing the mortgage payments of millions darn near overnight!

Chicago's outspoken & unconventional consumer advocate, financial expert, and 'Miracle worker,' Scott Tucker, is now putting to work this safe, and somewhat 'Secret' federal government program (that 'they' don't want us to know about) to beat the 'fat cat' lenders at their own game! Saving folks with "FHA" mortgages from financial hardship!

Tucker says, "the credit crunch, problems with the dollar, and rising energy prices, mean it's getting terribly hard for everyday, hard-working, cash-strapped American home owners to make their housing and other monthly payments!"

He continues, "And right now, a lot of folks with FHA mortgages feel like they're trapped because they think that they can't get their FHA mortgage payments reduced. And they don't want to sell their house either. But thing is, there is one little-known, and quiet-kept federal government program that can help you, that 'they' don't want you to know about!

"Right now, millions of folks with FHA mortgages are in real danger of going 30-days delinquent on their FHA mortgage payments. So they need to act now to take advantage of this 'Secret' government program, before they are ruled ineligible! Time is of the essence.

Section A, Page 2   **CONSUMER FINANCE**   Januar

"If you already have an 'FHA' mortgage…"

Or, the government could just pull the plug on the whole program! says Tucker.

But Tucker has a loud & clear message of hope for folks with FHA mortgages. "It's NOT the end yet for the vast majority of folks with FHA mortgages. Because I've uncovered a Secret government program that quickly & easily puts your mortgage payments back to where they should be. You no longer can be abused by your mortgage company and their unfair interest rates! That is, as long as

- ☐ "Are you're a home owner with an 'FHA' mortgage already? That you've had for at least 6 months?"
- ☐ "Are you NOT currently 30-days delinquent on your 'FHA' mortgage? Nor on any _federally-insured_ student loans?"
- ☐ "Do you want to pay LESS on your mortgage each & every month? And get your finances back under YOUR control?"

you can answer 'YES' to my 3 brain-dead easy questions? Then I can use this safe federal government program to slash your mortgage payments darn near overnight!"

"If you can answer 'yes' to each of those 3 questions, then you're home free!" Tucker exclaims. "And best of all, this safe federal government program does NOT involve any hassles such as credit counseling, bankruptcy, and you do NOT have to sell your house! This safe federal government program simply makes your mortgage company cry 'uncle' and cough-up lower mortgage payments for you from here on out!"

"With this safe federal government program, you're NOT 'zapping' equity from your house, and you won't be adding years to your mortgage payments either! So you're not being 'suckered' into one of those ridiculous long-term 'solutions'! And, in most cases it doesn't even matter if you have a second mortgage on your house! Best of all, this is a safe federal government program! It's just that you're mortgage company won't tell you it exists!" says Tucker.

Tucker continues, "So long as you're not 30-days behind on your FHA mortgage payments right now, I can get you into this Secret federal government program! See, right now, the door on this program is open to you! But it's vital that you get started now, before you get 30-days behind!"

"Folks who I've helped to use this program have had their mortgage payments slashed! That free-up all kinds of cash for them each & every month! All of the sudden, you've got cash in

"I can help you now, but please don't wait until I can't help any longer!" says Tucker

your pocket every month, finally giving you 'room to breathe!' And that makes it easier to pay your other bills on time too!" says Tucker.

"I know that when money first starts to get tight that folks naturally start to feel afraid, anxious, even depressed, and then just want to do nothing. But doing nothing is the worst thing you can do!" Tucker insists.

"You have to ask for help now, while this safe government program is still available. Don't wait for things to get worse, or for the government to yank this program! So long as you get call me now, while your payments are less than 30-days behind, I can and will fix it for you! And I can do it darn near overnight! And you get almost instant peace of mind' and a whole bunch of cash left over at the end of every month!" says Tucker.

"It's not hard for you to do this either! Oh, it's a bunch of work for me, to be sure, but darn near effortless for you! In fact, I do it all for you, and before you know it, you're out of the mess you find yourself in, and you're sleeping soundly again!" he says.

Tucker is adamant, "you have to take the first step. After that, it's as easy as falling off a log. I know it seems like the easiest thing to do is to just ignore it and wait for it to magically 'go away', but it won't if you won't ask for help!

'Oh, and there's one last thing,' Tucker says, "although this is a safe government program, and it exists today, you and I both know they could change this program at any time …maybe even making it unavailable. Could happen tomorrow, next week, next month. Who knows, crazier things have happened!"

Tucker continues, "and if you want until they close this program, it could be gone forever, they don't have to bring it back. And then I wouldn't be able to help you! And neither would anyone else! So even if you think you're gonna make it without my help, you should call me today to get this started, before it's too late!"

"For those who've waited for too long, and who are currently 30-days

behind on their FHA mortgage, well, it's too late for them now, and the federal government will not let me help them now. It's so sad for them, and I really don't want this to needlessly happen to anyone else!" Tucker says.

He puts it this way, "if you're finding it harder & harder to pay your bills, but you're not 30-days behind on your FHA mortgage right now, then you need to get my help now, before it's too late! It doesn't make any sense to fret and worry, when in just a few days you could be sleeping soundly again, knowing you're back on the right track!"

"I know you're probably a proud person. You don't want to have to ask for help. But there's really nothing to be 'ashamed' of, because just about everyone is in the same spot right now. It's not your fault. It's only your fault if you allow it to continue the way it is today. Nothing, is harder than struggling through it all by yourself," Tucker says.

He continues, "the saddest call I ever get is from someone who waited until they were more than 30-days behind on their FHA mortgage, and now finds they can't make their mortgage payment. All they have to look forward to is the sheriff at their door. With the locksmith and the moving crew in tow."

"Calls like that just break my heart. But when that happens, when folks call me when they're 30-days behind on their FHA mortgage, it's too late for me to fix it for them. Crazy, I know, but that's the government for ya. They'll let me help you now, but not later," he says.

"To ask Scott Tucker for help with this safe government program, call his 24-hour free "eavesdrop" hotline! There won't be a live person to 'bother' you there, you'll just 'listen in' to his 100% free recorded message. The number to call is 1-800-xxx-xxxx, then press 1, then enter extension 9000!

Or if you prefer to research Mr. Tucker online, you may do so at www.MemberWebsite.com. There, you'll find even more information on him, and on this 'Secret' safe, government program! Complete with case studies of other folks, just like you, that he's helped! Best of all, you can even **apply online** for his help right away! Remember the quicker you act, the quicker he can help you!

Or, to reach Scott Tucker at his office, you can call 773-xxx-xxxx, or call him toll-free at 1-800-xxx-xxxx! (Some use the toll-free number to call from work, from the pay phone, or from the neighbor's, after the phones been shut-off!)

One things for certain, sitting still won't solve your problems, but Scott Tucker will!

MAKE THE BALANCE CHECKING

By Peter Kenny

Having a checking account of your money and po checking account, but not know how to balan to bounced checks and Here are some simple s checking account.

Know where you are a you are at with your c records. You need to be with something else in month balance. The b check register that com Do not put it off. When the mail, open it and re always better to examine

Come i
see our
line of
in time

information on the sta your register the less li Make sure that you ch statement against your checks that have come have not come in and If you have an accoun balance, make sure the summary. Most people but consumers with in who must maintain in want to make sure they stay in compliance wit Another good way to management skills is capabilities, if you have easy way to find out w day to day. It is also a checks that have not outstanding. Online b

Chapter Eight
Marketing

When I say that you can create for yourself who you want to be today and not tomorrow, what I mean is that your borrowers' *perception* of you is actually created by your very own marketing. There's no sort of rap sheet credit report or background check that they do on you. They simply read the marketing that you've provided to them about you, and that forms their view of you. So, for better or for worse, you do it to yourself!

Of course, the point of the marketing that you provide them is to give them a favorable opinion of you. It should build you up as a guru, and as someone that they can trust. Someone with a proven track record with your past borrowers. That's why I'm always confused, befuddled, and baffled when other mortgage brokers choose to market in the me-too fashion against the other mortgage guys and talk about rate and fee. They totally miss the point of talking about *who they are* and how they've helped people just like this new prospect in the past. And, nearly 100% of mortgage brokers fail to use past borrower testimonials! Yet, in direct mail of any type, for any industry, mailings "split-tested" against each other, with and without testimonials, repeatedly prove that testimonials *double* response rates! Look at what the diet food companies do. And the acne cures. They all use testimonials, because otherwise the promises they make are not believable in the prospects eyes.

Your identity with your borrowers plays a very important role for you. And you're the only person that determines exactly what their perception of you is. There's no one else; they don't know what to think of you except for what *you* tell them with your marketing. And, if you simply fail to impress them, they will take no notice of you at all, which is a death sentence to your mortgage business. One crazy example of all this is, when you direct them to your website via an offline technique, like a mailing, they don't now Google you, they only go to your site. And, they somehow think that they've now done their due diligence on you! Yet all they've done, is go to your own website, and read what you've written about yourself! It's funny, but that's the way they view it. This is a case of activity masquerading as accomplishment, in their minds. This is a very powerful technique.

"A Mortgage Broker Walks into a Bar and Everyone Yells, 'Norm!'"

I have a little saying: "The industry 'Norm' sits next to Cliff Claven at the end of the bar." In fact, the industry norms aren't as useful as the Norm on *Cheers,* because at least *that* Norm is *supposed* to be funny. In the mortgage business, the foolish things most do, just because they see others doing the same, are no laughing matter. It's why most fail in this business. Simply put, it's a herd mentality. Herd mentality serves us well in the wild, to keep us safe from danger, and to make sure we don't starve, out there by ourselves. But in a competitive "Lone Ranger" business environment like the mortgage business, in a capitalistic society such as ours, we're each responsible for our own outcomes. No matter what any liberal politician might tell you, the *only* person who's going to help you is *you.* The government simply doesn't have the resources, or the ability, to "make" you a millionaire. You *might* get by with their "help," you might get welfare, you might get what passes for their version of healthcare, you might get a place to stay, but that's all you're going to get—the absolute *minimum* in life. They'll keep you alive, but not much else. If just getting by isn't for you, which I think it probably isn't, since you're reading this book, and since you got into the mortgage business to make big money, then you need to become damned serious about *violating* industry norms.

Another reason to do the *opposite* of what most people in the mortgage industry are doing is that most people in the mortgage business don't make any real money.

The average income in the mortgage business, for loan officers, is only $55,000 I guess to some people that's a "good amount of money," but I live in Chicago, and for $55,000 a year you can't do much of anything. My idea of a good income in the mortgage business is, as I've said before, somewhere around a $500,000.00 dollars a year. And that's possible even in some Podunk markets. One of my members, a gentleman in Wichita, Kansas, is, in the middle of this current mortgage funk, just like the rest of us. In February 2008, however, he made $80,000.00 using my mortgage marketing system. He's getting 5 points a deal, and the loan amounts there are only around $100,000 a piece, so in order to be making $80,000.00 in a month, he's doing quite well. I mean, that's $960,000.00 a year, in Wichita, Kansas, and in the middle of the "credit crunch!"

There is a fundamental problem with the strategy of following "industry Norm's," which is that you are going to get the same results that everybody else is getting, and everybody else's results are no good. This'd be great if everyone in the industry was making money, but in a down time if you do what everyone else does, you're not going to make any money at all. And even in boom times, following the herd won't serve you well either. It seems that everyone gets into the mortgage business because they know of somebody who made a lot of money in the business. They think the answer is simply getting into the right business. It's *not*. There's no "good business," and there's no "bad business." I'm sure the mortgage business is better than many others. I mean, I'd rather be a mortgage broker than a roofer, but there's really no good or bad business. The industry you're in alone doesn't make or break you. What makes or breaks you is what *you* do as far as *marketing*.

The other thing that will make you successful in the mortgage business is high fees. Having borrowers who are desensitized to high fees, through the use of effective de-commoditizing mortgage marketing systems, is essential. Beyond that, you need to keep your past borrowers corralled, by fencing them in, with a Past Borrower Retention System®, just like the one my broker members use.

The smartest strategy for mortgage marketing is to have a set of proven marketing pieces, such as a direct mail piece, a freestanding insert ("FSI,") and maybe 2 or 3 proven niche publication display ads, in niche publications, where your best borrowers are already found. In fact, I supply my member brokers with these ads and a list of the niche publications to run them in. Some of these ads return as much as $52 in fee income to every $1 spent running the ads! This way, every day, even in the middle of the night, even on weekends, you're getting loan applications in your e-mail. All you have to do then is figure out what you think the property is worth, and there are several easy ways to do that online, without having to talk to the applicant. Then you can pull a credit report, and have the folks prequalified. In fact, you can get this systematized, to where your *assistant* takes the inbound lead e-mail transcript, and does all this for you. Your assistant can then get a real comp from a real appraiser for you, and they can even work up the whole deal based upon the info they've just gathered. So, using my system, the first time you bother with talking to the new borrowers, is when your assistant hands you the fully worked-up deal to pitch.

There's really no reason for *you* to have *any* involvement (or work to do) before you call back the borrower to pitch them on the deal.

The Top 5

The top 5 marketing techniques I've found that work in a mortgage brokerage are direct mailings, freestanding inserts, display ads in niche publications, door knockers, and voice broadcasts to past borrowers...

...as part of the Past Borrower Retention System®. If you had to start from scratch and create them all, this would obviously take a lot of work, experimentation, lost time and lost money. That's why I provide all of this, turnkey, to my member brokers. It's plug-and-play, and if necessary, I tweak it for your specific market. For instance, for Canadian member brokers. For more information on this automated marketing system that I provide to my member brokers, please go to **www.MortgageMarketingGenius.com**.

I have several successful marketing pieces. One example is called "The 'Mr. X' Letter," which is a direct response marketing piece sent to borrowers on a certain mailing list. I have others such as tear sheets—which are fake newspaper articles sent to those same folks—and display ads in certain niche publications that my borrowers happen to read, but where no other mortgage ads appear. And, even when they read the ad we use, it appears to be an article about my member broker, so they don't even realize they're reading an ad, and they also don't realize my member broker is a mortgage guy at all. You can also use my tear sheet direct mail pieces as freestanding inserts in shopper papers, such as *Thrifty Nickel, The Shopping Guide, Penny Saver,* and in card deck mailings, such as Val-Pak, Money Mailer, and ADVO. My member brokers are also provided with very unusual looking doorknockers. They are templated, just like everything else I provide to you, so that you can simply plug in your name, using my online marketing ordering site, that's provided only to my member brokers, in their exclusive marketing areas. I have a layout person and printer that fulfill your marketing order.

Not only do members get marketing systems that work, but I also exclude things that don't work, so they don't waste their time and money testing any "dogs" themselves. One thing that I found not to work very well were Yellow Pages ads. Even a very good Yellow Pages ad, in the mortgage section, isn't going to make you money, because that's where the *rate and fee shoppers* go. They are already in the "mortgage guy" frame of mind, and I've found it impossible to get them out of that mindset, no matter what the advertising copy says.

Another marketing media I would avoid is Google AdWords and other pay-per-click services. Don't bother buying terms like "mortgage refinance Chicago" because I found that while I could generate loan applications for about $10 a piece with this method, I couldn't close them, because they were applying with everyone else online, too, including LendingTree, plus they were entering their phone number, which then caused the trigger lead guys to stalk them as well. So the whole thing turned out to be a waste of time and money. Since I have already tested the Yellow Pages and pay-per-click ads for you, with top-notch "non-mortgage guy" ad copy, and shown them not to work in my own brokerage, you don't have to waste your time and money on them. These are the kind of time and money savings you get from my program.

We've tested, and been surprised by how well my doorknockers have done for my member brokers. It's kind of funny that they turned out to be so hot, because it was just a, "Hey, why not try this in our hot neighborhoods?" idea. And it's done very, very well! My unusual looking, non-mortgage guy doorknockers should be used in your "high-end Homer Simpson" neighborhoods where you already get a lot of loans, and a lot of cooperative borrowers that you like working with. Think high-end blue collar, low-end white collar. Good home values, good loan amounts, nice fees.

Effective mortgage marketing is all about the approach.

If you can approach borrowers *without* talking about a mortgage, and get people who wouldn't normally raise their hands for a mortgage to do so, then in a sense, you have opened the door to trust and the promise of having solutions to their problems. In the end, they are going to get a mortgage, have their problems solved, and be very happy with you. And you'll see referrals increase dramatically as well. They'll even describe you to their friends as some kind of miracle worker, never describing you as a mortgage guy, which is very, very nice!

Summary:

- The top 5 marketing techniques are: direct mailings, freestanding inserts, display ads in niche publications, door knockers, and voice broadcasts to past borrowers.
- Don't use pay-per-click Internet ads to attract mortgage borrowers.

Chapter Nine
It Doesn't Have to Be Hard Work for It to Work

Your chances of success in the mortgage business are just as poor as your chances of success anywhere else. You might be able to get by, but in the mortgage business you're not working on salary. You might receive minimum wage so your broker doesn't get sued for violating the minimum wage law, but minimum wage is poverty. It's really not a reason to get into the mortgage business, and it's certainly not financial incentive to stay.

To me, success in the mortgage business is a six-figure income, which on the very low end would be $100,000.00 a year. On the higher end, it's not improbable at all for a loan officer to do $1,000,000.00 a year, providing he has a mortgage marketing system and some degree of delegation of the grunt work.

A number of my broker members, in different parts of the country, even in some Podunk markets, have been able to easily do $400,000.00 or $500,000.00 a year, while only working 20 to 25 hours a week. Now, I think that's a pretty successful outcome for somebody in the mortgage business, or any business for that matter, but it just wouldn't be possible, the big money and the short hours, without implementing a mortgage marketing *system* that works while you don't!

When I first got started in the mortgage business, I understood salesmanship, and was quickly, very good at it. But salesmanship is not an automated marketing system. It was 3½ years later when my broker fired me, that I had to create *my own* mortgage marketing system, and to do that, I had to become a *very* serious student of how that all works.

So I studied the direct response marketing systems of several different companies, in industries *other* than the mortgage category, which is the *smart* way to build something that really *works*. I read 100-year-old books from the old masters of direct response marketing. It may surprise you to learn that direct mail marketing has existed as far back as the Civil War.

There are several ways to learn about direct response marketing. To start, you're going to need to read a whole lot of books on direct response marketing, from all sorts of sources. On top of all the reading, there are quite a few direct marketing seminars and copywriting seminars you'll need to attend. For instance, I went to a $5,000.00 per head seminar taught by the late, great Gary Halbert, and you just can't get Gary anymore. Then you'll have to try your hand at writing sales letters, and then testing them, by spending a whole lot of time and money mailing them, and seeing how they do. It's important to understand, that to be a successful copywriter you need to *first* be a successful salesman. If you've never sold something face-to-face, you'll probably never become a good copywriter, and you'll probably have to hire that out, and hope you get someone who understands your prospect.

If you want a shortcut, the best thing I can tell you is to plug into an existing mortgage marketing system that's been proven to work.

The educational materials I provide outside of this book are bundled into my mortgage marketing, coaching, and consulting membership program. You can find out more about that at www.MortgageMarketingGenius.com.

I have a very strong imagination, and that's a very important thing, that makes me able to take something from one industry, and apply it to another. Some folks don't have the wild imagination it takes to do that. Obviously, the best and easiest solution is to pay somebody else for the outcome that you want.

Done for You Services

As a member of my Tucker Mortgage Marketing System®, you'll have a login and password for my mortgage marketing website. The site will plug you into a network of vendors and enable you to order any of the direct response mortgage marketing materials you need for your mortgage business.

You'll have access to all the direct response marketing materials I've mentioned in this book, personalized for you, and then printed and shipped to you. If direct mail, they come to you in a big UPS box, ready for you to mail from your local post office as needed. By joining my program, you will be able to push a few buttons and have things set up for you by the vendors in my network. It's as easy as could be.

Coaching is an essential element in any endeavor. You can't be truly *great* in any field without a good coach. When I was in high school, I played hockey, and even though I started playing hockey when I was 7 years old, I never could have obtained the level of skill or accomplishment without good *coaching*. It was the same thing when I was in the Navy; we had *coaches*: company commanders in boot camp, instructors in "A" School, and a section leader at my base in Scotland. We had *coaches* all the way through.

What's unusual about the mortgage business, compared to other fields, is that oftentimes you're given no supervision at all! You're shown a desk, handed a phone, and told to somehow figure something out—and not to call anybody on the Do Not Call list! You're supposed to talk to all your relatives, and refinance them, and then go talk to some realtors to figure out how to somehow make some money. Even if you're fortunate enough to work with a broker who has a direct response marketing system set up for you, *their* system is all about *rates and fees,* and it sets up you up to fail, due to price shopping.

If you are smart enough to work with a broker who actually has a *real* mortgage marketing system that doesn't present the mortgage as a *commodity,* the problem is getting a small commission split. You'd have plenty of borrowers and probably be able to get the rates and fees up, but then you'd be giving the majority of the fees back to the broker. So to really have *independence,* you need to have *control* over the mortgage marketing system yourself.

As I mentioned in the beginning, it's important to have a mastermind group, like Napoleon Hill wrote in *Think and Grow Rich.* What's sad about the mortgage business, or really any businesses, is that if you have something that's *working,* you're afraid to tell any *other* mortgage broker in your town about it, because you're afraid he'll steal your idea and all your borrowers. As a result, everybody lives in ignorance because no one talks to each other.

What's exciting about my mortgage coaching program is not only are all of my members able to use my materials, they're the *only* guy in their area able to do so. Something else that happens is my member broker from say, Tulsa, Oklahoma, can share his secrets with the guy in say, Albany, New York, and so on. This way there are never any 2 members in any 1 area. Everybody freely shares information, to make all of us stronger, rather than keeping their mouths shut and not spreading any of the new techniques that work.

For those who have their own mortgage marketing system going already, but need a refresher course, I offer consulting on a case-by-case basis. However, I usually limit consulting days to about 1 per month, and the fees are high enough that you'd be better off joining my Tucker Mortgage Marketing System®, and using those resources and tools to enhance or replace certain elements of your system.

Final Thoughts

The #1 thing to understand about the mortgage business is that the majority is always wrong. Eighty percent of the people make 20% of the money. If you want to be in the top 20% of the top 20%, who really make a whole lot of money in the mortgage business, then you must do the *opposite* of what everybody else is doing. That means you have to have a mortgage marketing system that gets you direct response from borrowers; you need to cut realtors out of the whole process, stop doing purchase deals, and instead focus on refi's. Focus on niches *within* the refi market such as the Fannie/Freddie Prime ARM resets, the FHA Streamline refi's, and something I consider a refi, even though others may not—the reverse mortgage.

It is within niches like these that the best opportunities exist for the mortgage broker, but it is only through proper marketing that these niches become *accessible*. My Tucker Mortgage Marketing System® offers you everything I've described in this book, all done for you, saving you time, money, and effort. Visit www.MortgageMarketingGenius.com to change the way you do business—and the way you do life!

Summary:

- Hard work isn't always better than finding an easier way.
- You need coaching in anything you do.
- You need to "MasterMind" with others with like goals.

Keep an eye out for Scott's next book,
**Reverse Mortgages
...from Z to A**

TreeNeutral

Advantage Media Group is proud to be a part of the Tree Neutral™ program. Tree Neutral offsets the number of trees consumed in the production and printing of this book by taking proactive steps such as planting trees in direct proportion to the number of trees used to print books. To learn more about Tree Neutral, please visit **www.treeneutral.com**. To learn more about Advantage Media Group's commitment to being a responsible steward of the environment, please visit **www.advantagefamily.com/green**

Marketing for Mortgage Brokers is available in bulk quantities at special discounts for corporate, institutional, and educational purposes. To learn more about the special programs Advantage Media Group offers, please visit **www.KaizenUniversity.com** or call 1.866.775.1696.

Advantage Media Group is a leading publisher of business, motivation, and self-help authors. Do you have a manuscript or book idea that you would like to have considered for publication? Please visit **www.amgbook.com**